Uncommon: Transcending the Lies of the Mental Health Industry

Dan Desmarques

Published by 22 Lions Publishing, 2020.

Table of Contents

Copyright Page..1

Introduction..3

Chapter 1: Why Do They Lie to You?..5

Chapter 2: Why is There So Much Ignorance in The World?............7

Chapter 3: Where Did They Get Their Ideas From?........................11

Chapter 4: Why is Mental Health Important in Today's Society?...15

Chapter 5: How Do You Deal With Unconscious People?..............19

Chapter 6: How Does Culture Affect Mental Health?....................21

Chapter 7: What Can Be Done For People Suffering With Mental Illness?..23

Chapter 8: Why Are Most People Predictable?...............................27

Chapter 9: What is The Line Between Sanity and Insanity?...........29

Chapter 10: Why People Sometimes Prefer Lies to The Truth?......33

Chapter 11: Why Does Misinterpretation Happen?.......................35

Chapter 12: Why Losing Friends Can Be a Blessing?.....................37

Chapter 13: What Does it Mean to Lack Empathy?.......................39

Chapter 14: What is Metacognitive Therapy?................................43

Chapter 15: Why You Should Never Stop Loving Yourself?...........47

Chapter 16: How to Attract More Opportunities in Your Life?......51

Chapter 17: What is The True Meaning of Evil?............................55

Chapter 18: Why Do We Need Introspection?...............................59

Chapter 19: What Are The Benefits of Self-Love?..........................61

Chapter 20: How to Stop Running Away From Yourself? 63

Chapter 21: How to Overcome The Illusion of Fear? 67

Chapter 22: Why are People Afraid of Change? 71

Chapter 23: How Do You Focus on Solutions Rather Than Problems?........ 75

Chapter 24: How Can You Feel Younger and Have More Energy?................ 79

Chapter 25: What is The Difference Between Competence and Capacity?... 83

Chapter 26: Why Some People Love Conflict and Drama? 87

Chapter 27: Why is There Evil? 91

Chapter 28: How Do Brain Waves Influence Our Emotional State? 95

Chapter 29: Why is Point of View So Important For Our Well-being? 99

Chapter 30: What Types of People You Cannot Help? 103

Chapter 31: Is Insanity Contagious? 105

Chapter 32: How Can a Subgroup Impact Our Mental Health?.............. 109

Chapter 33: How To Deal With Negative Thoughts? 113

Chapter 34: Can Love Be a Healing Force? 115

Chapter 35: Why Is Chaos In Your Life Essential To True Growth? 117

Chapter 36: Is Jealousy a Symptom of Psychiatric Disorder? 119

Chapter 37: Why Life is a Mirror Reflecting Your Inner World? 123

Chapter 38: What are the Levels of Our Hierarchy of Needs? 127

Chapter 39: How Does Mental Illness Affect Behavior? 131

Chapter 40: Why is Mental Health a Social Problem? 133

Chapter 41: Can Depression Prevent You From Achieving Goals? 135

Chapter 42: What are The Benefits of Using Your Imagination?................139

Chapter 43: How Setting Goals Can Help Your Mental Health?.................143

Chapter 44: Why Do We Try to Fit in?..147

Chapter 45: Can Discrimination Be Harmful to Your Mental Health?........151

Chapter 46: Why Do We Feel Rejected?...155

Chapter 47: Why Do We Feel Lonely?..157

Chapter 48: Why Loneliness Can Make You Successful?..........................161

Chapter 49: Why Do We Need Friends?...165

Chapter 50: How to Be a Better Person?..169

Chapter 51: Is Happiness a State of Mind?...173

Chapter 52: Why Do We Separate Ourselves From Others?.....................177

Chapter 53: Does Psychotherapy Have Side Effects?...............................181

Chapter 54: Is Self-Absorption The Root of All Psychological Evil?..........185

Chapter 55: How to Protect Yourself From Emotional Abuse?.................189

Chapter 56: How to Properly Judge People?..193

Chapter 57: Can Society Contribute to Poor Mental Health?...................197

Chapter 58: What are The Stages of Moral Development?......................201

Chapter 59: How to Evaluate Moral Development?................................205

Chapter 60: What are The Effects of Immorality?...................................209

Chapter 61: How to Be Uncommon and Moral?.....................................213

Copyright Page.

Uncommon: Transcending the Lies of the Mental Health Industry

By Dan Desmarques

Copyright © Dan Desmarques, 2020 (1st Ed.) All Rights Reserved.

Introduction.

We trust doctors and researches in the field of mental health out of lack of choices. But the psychiatric industry is intrinsically connected to the government and the lobbies of the pharmaceutical corporations.

As you will se in this book, much of what should be known about mental health is kept hidden from the general public. And on the other hand, a lot of what is promoted intends to destroy the natural state of mind of the majority of the people who go through these methods.

Most of the population of the world is willing to cooperate with the system promoted by those in control, for it is easier than to oppose and revolt. To oppose the mainstream solutions is now an act of rebellion seen as insanity or conspiracy. As such, the elimination of dissents, by discrediting them, is easily put in practice due to the ignorance of the many.

The vast majority of the population lacks answers that can help them in coping with life as it is right now, and in overcoming their personal problems. Many are already mentally broken and unable to think effectively.

It is for these, that seek alternatives and want to rehabilitate themselves, but also become more resilient and capable of handling different types of difficulties, that this book was created.

Chapter 1: Why Do They Lie to You?

Most solutions, offered to an increasingly insane world, are basically leading to death faster than expected.

When visiting a psychologist, patients typically tend to be immediately convinced that the origin of their problem lies in their childhood, which leads to endless months of appointments going nowhere, most likely with the intention of increasing profits for the psychologist than focus on the needs of the patient.

It is difficult to see anything different from this reality because doctors and therapists would lose their job and license if they approached their patients from a different viewpoint, and despite the many crimes that a vast number of them commit within the walls of their clinics and that often go unnoticed.

The United States loses approximately $100 billion (€81.5 billion) to health care fraud each year. Up to $20 billion (€15.7 billion) of this is due to fraudulent practices in the mental health industry.

In Australia, health care fraud and patient over-servicing has cost taxpayers up to $330 million (€226 million) a year.

In Ontario, Canada, psychotherapist Michael Bogart was sentenced to 18 months in jail for defrauding the government of almost $1 million (€815,993).

Mark Schiller, president of the American Association of Physicians and Surgeons, admitted to "Have frequently seen psychiatrists diagnose patients with a range of psychiatric diagnoses that aren't justified, to obtain [insurance] reimbursements."

However, the mental health industry, to a vast degree is never made accountable. In fact, as former president of the American Psychiatric Association (APA), Paul Fink, arrogantly admitted: "It is the task of the APA to protect the earning power of psychiatrists."

According to Jan Eastgate — President of the Citizens Commission on Human Rights International, "The mental health monopoly has practically zero accountability and zero liability for its failures. This has allowed psychiatrists and psychologists to commit far more than just financial fraud.

The roster of crimes committed by these "professionals" ranges from fraud, drug offenses, rape and sexual abuse to child molestation, assault, manslaughter and murder."

In Lithuania, the world number one nation for suicides, most fail to notice that the psychologists and psychiatrists of the country are behind such horrible statistics. Never would one imagine that the high levels of suicide in one country could be linked to their own mental health "professionals", and yet, this is exactly what happens.

In a research conducted on this country in 2017, it was found that some of the psychologists actually persuade their patients to commit suicide.

In one particular case, a Lithuanian psychologist was recorded with a hidden camera, saying to her patient things like, "To think about suicide is normal" and "It is ok to smoke drugs and have promiscuous sex whenever you want", and also, "Let me know if you ever decide to kill yourself! Just give me a call before actually doing it."

When confronted with these affirmations and abuses, she refused to justify herself, insulted, cursed, and runaway. And yet, this monster, continues to practice behind closed doors and even giving courses to other psychologists.

Most government officials in Lithuania are too busy looking at the high alcohol consumption and the unemployment rate as the causes of the suicides, and meanwhile, everyone ignores the real cause in front of their nose.

In one interview with a Ukrainian Psychologist on the type of education given in Lithuania, she said: "It is the worse I have ever seen; many things they say are actually the complete opposite of what should be said to a person."

Chapter 2: Why is There So Much Ignorance in The World?

The imbecility of many psychologists comes, to a great extent, from the illusion passed unto them that they know how the mind works. As if rats and pigeons — the animals used in most of their research deductions — had all the wisdom in the world to explain the mind.

In effect, what most of what the psychologists — in all the cases I met personally, that can't even help themselves — end up doing, is selling a fraud in which they themselves want to believe.

This fraud is based on the idea that humans are nothing but animals that must be kept within the herd of society, as if the majority was the "normal".

I don't know how much the psychiatric patients, for example, under the supervision of the Portuguese Association of Patients with Schizophrenia, would believe their doctor, if they went on a club and saw the President crawling on the floor with the mask of a dog and having the best time of his life.

There are things that I have personally seen, which are just too hard to believe, even if you see them in front of you.

Psychiatrists and psychologists are some of the sickening people I have ever encountered.

Their self-belief comes mostly from the aura that their medical field gives them. But a normal research on the field of Mental Health would allow anyone observing four facts:

- Psychiatry is based on a manual called DSM — Diagnostic and Statistical Manual of Mental Disorders, which has been changed over the past sixty years to suit governmental purposes;

- Most so-called psychological illnesses are created after the Pharmaceutical Industry launches a new drug in the market and not before;

- There's no scientific measurement showing how a mental illness can be related to an imbalance within the body or how a balance can be reestablished;

- There's absolutely no relevant statistical evidence proving uplifting results from the use of drugs or electroconvulsive therapies in the treatment of depression but there are many showing how these treatments lead to apathy and suicide, as well as physical illnesses.

Psychiatrists are so convinced of their own fraud, that they completely ignore that the most famous psychiatric drugs, like prozac and lithium, have compounds such as fluoride, commonly found in rat poison, and are known to produce the following effects:

- Arthritis;

- Chronic fatigue syndrome (CFS);

- Diabetes – worsening symptoms;

- Fibromyalgia (severe muscle weakness and/or pain with extremely sore spots on various bony areas);

- Food intolerances that seem to come and go ;

- Gastrointestinal problems – irritable bowel, nausea, diarrhea without apparent cause, heartburn and upper bowel pain;

- Heart palpitations and increased heart rate without exertion;

- Kidney disease – worsening symptoms, kidney stones;

- Teeth – loosening or needing to be extracted despite good hygiene and diet.

Often seems that the solution to a problem creates a bigger one. And shockingly, whenever I tell this to people, they refuse to believe. Because it's just too hard to assimilate that they went to a butcher rather than a healer to cure their mental problems.

They go with a depression, and leave with the subliminal promise of a cancer and a damaged brain thanks to the drug prescriptions.

Chapter 3: Where Did They Get Their Ideas From?

Just like the principles of modern psychology were developed during Second World War, and mainly with military purposes, psychiatry also started its first steps here, in this case by testing poisonous substances on victims of the holocaust. The main purpose was to find ways to diminish the response capability of a population during an invasion.

The more the population of the world is willing to cooperate with the system promoted by those who control it, the easier it is to proceed without rebellions and revolutions.

The same action has another advantage for this power elite and that is the diminishing of the world population. When tested by the Nazis, these drugs intended to kill secretly, which means leading to a slow death by disease while not allowing tracing back the cause. In particular, drugs given by psychiatrists, not only do this, but also tend to increase dependency and suicidal tendencies.

Most solutions given to an increasingly insane world population are basically leading to death faster than expected.

The tendency for psychologists to advise people to take antidepressants is also increasing, even though they are not doctors that can give prescriptions. But they do! Illegally!

The message transmitted is that taking a certain drug will help in dealing with the therapy, when in fact the main purpose is to create dependency in a drug that diminishes self-awareness and the capability to solve one's own problems.

If you visit a psychiatrist, on the other hand, such prescription will occur almost immediately after a subjective diagnosis, because, according to the DSM, any kind of personality can be medicated.

It is difficult to see anything differently because doctors and therapists would lose their job and license if they did otherwise. Their medical career depends in following specific procedures.

As students, therapists of the Mental Health Industry are programmed with a certain amount of beliefs which lead to things they end up assuming as facts, such as that nobody can be helped, and humans are just animals. To make sure such ideas are followed, their study includes a huge amount of experiences that have been manipulated, and in some cases never truly existed, that they then need to memorize for exams. The exams of these future mental health experts are nothing more than a regurgitation of procedures and results lacking effectiveness.

When given the chance to conduct their own scientific experiments, again, they are trapped inside the same dogma, with researches commonly leading to the same paradigm. Rats and pigeons are the basis of many of such experiments and Darwin's theory is behind the backing of their conclusions, even though the leading biologists of today know that such theory is wrong.

When an experiment is applied to a group of the population, the one chosen is typically poor or deprived of a proper existence, so that the results may again conduct to the idea that we are basically animals.

The only researches seen as useful, are those serving political and corporate purposes, and these are the ones which actually receive funds to be properly developed and applied.

Humanitarian researches promoting a united and uplifting spiritual society don't receive the same level of support. And if their results don't follow what has been found already, or contradict the mainstream agenda, these results are suppressed.

Few even dare to contradict Freud, Wundt and Pavlov these days, and, nevertheless, Freud was a Freemason, Wundt was a member of Skulls and Bones, and Pavlov was a member of Kharkov-kiev, all of them interconnected Secret Societies with their own agendas.

UNCOMMON: TRANSCENDING THE LIES OF THE MENTAL HEALTH INDUSTRY

If it wasn't for Freemasonry, Freud would never have developed psychotherapy, as the idea of a subconscious mind was already known and exposed in Hindu scripture and many other ancient religious texts.

Chapter 4: Why is Mental Health Important in Today's Society?

The main problem for everyone needing psychological help is related to a lack of options. Nobody knows who to ask for help anymore. Unfortunately, the solution today is for us to help ourselves.

There is information available in most libraries and in the internet on how to improve life and change lifestyle, but there must be an effort in searching for it. Most people are unwilling to take the necessary steps, especially when their psychological condition doesn't allow it.

There are, however, some basic things that, when applied, can lead to quick and positive changes. One of the most fundamental, is to take responsibility for our own results. Responsibility is the assuming that we're in control of our own life, problems and solutions.

Those that are mentally ill are unable to be responsible for their life, and this is often an excuse to put healthy individuals inside mental health hospitals, or to justify psychopathic tendencies. But interestingly enough, we're deprived from responsibility in school and later in our job, because we believe that obeying is more important than confronting reality independently.

Being responsible is not about accepting what is given to you, but rather about being the cause of all changes in life, instead of complaining, or finding justifications for a self-provoked condition.

This responsibility to change is then assumed as a knowing that, when something is wrong, a change is necessary, which is the opposite of accepting a given condition.

We are conditioned to obey at home, in school and later in our workplace, but this mental programming leads us to believe that changing is supposed to be avoided at all costs. And the truth is quite the contrary, as since primitive times man has changed land permanently for many different reasons, and only in more recent years have we stopped doing that, because, actually, it complicates the management of a nation, and that's why now we have borders, visas and passports.

The idea that we are conditioned by the environment shifts our mental thoughts inwards, towards guilt, resentment and even abasement. The opposite has to necessarily bring action to one's reality.

There's no solution without an act towards that. You will not find a solution by looking at your TV screen, or by thinking about the same problem repeatedly.

A solution will come when you do something about it or about yourself at least. And this requires a certain amount of movement in a specific direction. The actions then take their impact according to the emotions fueling them.

We do things for a reason and based on a reason. Our goals always need to match our beliefs. And the more they do, the more likely we are to achieve them, but also more self-encouraged and motivated we are to obtain them. And so, if this principle applies to mental health, and to heal depression, or a variety of many mental illnesses, and it truly does, we can assume the following:

- Emotions are the root cause of the mental illnesses;

- Emotions are the path towards healing from any mental condition.

How can we use them to heal?

The most simplistic approach consists in using our emotions to:

- Dream and envision a possibility into our future, namely, our own healing;

- Use our emotional awareness to reach for the past and confront our suffering and anger.

Any method that uses these principles succeeds.

So why is the mental health industry and religions such a disaster?

UNCOMMON: TRANSCENDING THE LIES OF THE MENTAL HEALTH INDUSTRY

Because they are in the business of having followers and milking them for money. It is not in their spectrum of possibilities to allow people to be independent. Therefore, they never go the whole way, or they keep people imprisoned to one of the aspects mentioned.

- The psychotherapist constantly digs into the past, but is apathetic to the dreams of the patient. Because after assuming that the patient has mental limitations, the goals of the therapist end up naturally being towards bringing this person into a social norm, rather than beyond it;

- The priest quite often attaches the dreams of his followers to the promise of eternal life, to keep them from finding their own heaven.

Our emotions are very important in dealing with life, and knowing how to take a break, enjoy the sun, smell the flowers and listen to the birds, can be more positive for mental health than taking a drug.

The problem with this path of solutions is that it demands a choice, a decision to change, and, if the individual doesn't want or doesn't believe in change, then that person will sink deeper into the waters of his self-beliefs, making it harder to be saved from his mental condition.

Chapter 5: How Do You Deal With Unconscious People?

It is interesting to notice that psychology and psychotherapy often refer to their experiences with human beings as being representative of how a society should be, while in fact describing a majority that they recognize to be insane. That's why they can find a definition of abnormal behavior for anyone representing that same majority.

How can we then expect to cure people based on studies made with insane individuals? Because that's what the majority is — insane.

We live in a highly insane world, where most people are actually either neurotic or psychotic without realizing it, or at a mental level that is not balanced anymore. It is just a matter of time for that majority to fall into a situation that is not sustainable any longer.

All we need is some virus, mass unemployment or a global war, to see the demons within them in full display. Because, you see, for example, the Polish are still, in their great majority, a bunch of nazis, the Danish and the Dutch are still racist, and Germans still consider themselves superior to other nations.

What changed? Our perceptions of ourselves did! We use now the political correct to police ourselves and deny our own awareness, no matter how many times we are insulted and offended due to the color of our skin.

Europeans are still a bunch of racist nazis, they are still xenophobic, and they still think like little tribes, always ready for war in the name of a flag, a stupid dumb idea someone invented, because they are still the same lunatic morons in 2020 as they were in 1920 or 1520.

Nothing has changed! But people believe it did. And so, the insistence in this lunacy of denying the obvious, keeps them in the "never happened land".

What do I mean by that? I mean that, when someone gets insulted because he was born in a certain country deemed inferior, or has a certain skin color, others blame the victim rather than the aggressor. They think the victim must have done something for the abuser to react in such a way. And this is how Europeans systematically maintain the "it's the jewish fault" in their mind.

They didn't change! It's the same ideology as always. Except that now they don't blame the jews because someone told them they can't. They blame the Arabs, the Africans, and the South Americans, they blame the gypsies, they blame the Russians, and anyone else they can. In other words, nothing has changed. Because they are still insane as a continent.

How can this insanity change if those in power and in positions of influence, such as the teachers, the politicians and the governmental officials and institutions, such as the Universities, continue to replicate the same mindset?

Those who don't suffer from mental disorders or even depression are usually being supported by a good social life and a stable job. It is the idea that they are integrated into the system that makes them believe nothing is wrong with them.

Most people actually believe that by having friends and a job, they hold immunity to any mental disorder, and that this represents a status associated with being normal.

That's not true! Reason why, when they lose their job, family or friends, they then become deeply depressed. They have lost the only things that allowed them to hide from the truth. But these individuals were already in a high risk of depression before such events occurred.

The justifications that we fabricate for ourselves, to deny accepting that which we can't confront, are the source of all forms of insanity.

Chapter 6: How Does Culture Affect Mental Health?

Europeans are very sick as a continent! To talk about the European culture is to address insanity at a larger scale.

When we look at the concentration camps of Auschwitz, for example, we wonder how could humans be so atrocious and imbecile in the past, and fail to see that these persons are still here, in the same place, and never vanished. That evil never died. The Polish people are extremely racist. And they would exterminate others again, if given the chance under the right conditions. They still believe that any aggression against outsiders is justified.

Could we then say that destroying Poland is an act of evil?

You see, that's the thing people don't seem to understand. Evil against evil is not evil; it's called solving a problem.

The destruction of Europe as a continent of nations, is not only necessary, but imperative, if we wish to eradicate xenophobia and racism. As a matter of fact, xenophobia and racism can only vanish once we create a new world order. And the ignorance of those who are against it, comes from the dual thinking they have, that if those who want the new world order are motivated by self-interest, then this order must be bad.

This is due to the lack of capacity of the humans on earth to think beyond the patterns of dual thinking — a bidimensional approach to reality. These individuals are under-evolved to a very great extent.

Evolution comes as a development of the mind, rather than a positioning towards one or another aspect of the policies being developed. This said, a new world order is necessary to end differentiations and flags, for without it, xenophobia, racism and nationalism will hardly disappear. They will more likely lead to more wars.

We believe that, if we do what others do, everything will be fine, not noticing that when the blind leads the blind, both are still blind and both are led astray.

People trust too much their politicians, who have nothing more than the illusion of knowing what they are doing, and know just as much as any other common person. And that's what democracy really is — the equalization of stupidity.

Democracy is basically another word for Communism, which is another way for the right to equalize the stupid in a hierarchy of power.

Nobody is ever prepared for leadership except those who are raised within a monarchy.

I am not saying, however, that monarchy is the right path, for a monarch needs an empire to rule. I am saying that democracy is an illusion.

Just as a an engineer must study how to build bridges, and the teacher must be taught on how to educate, the ruler must be shown how to rule. To ignore this is to consider anyone can be a doctor and anyone can be an engineer. Which is a widespread belief that has led to quite a lot of incompetence on the workplace.

Chapter 7: What Can Be Done For People Suffering With Mental Illness?

Mental illness comes from the deprivation of life. It is that simple. The complexities that derive from it are basically an expression of the inability to live such a life.

We often feel depressed first, as a warning of our body to let us know that we're not living life properly, and as much as physical pain tells us that we've come too close to a heated or sharp object.

We need to feel depressed so that we may understand happiness, just like we need to do mistakes to understand how to do things well.

However, we deprive ourselves from life when choosing to spend time watching movies and in front of a computer screen, or when spending too much time in bed, when choosing to do what others want for us, instead of what we should be doing, or instead of what we would like to do.

People get depressed because they basically don't have a life of their own with free will. Their life is to sleep, go to work, type in chartrooms and blogs, and watch movies. And you must live your own life, not somebody else's life, or what someone else wants you to live.

Most of the problems that people have, come from above, in the form of systems that are ideological and mainstream to a whole of society but idealized by their own governments and institutions. Many of the people suffering depression don't really have reasons to be depressed, but they are, because of the common need to fit in, adapt and belong.

Most of peoples' problems, either they are financial, emotional or mental, can be, quite simply, resumed to the need to fit in. And if most of 90% of physical illnesses have a mental origin, we can very well say the same about these. I.e., the need to fit in is making people sick.

Some estimate that the percentage is lower, but there may come a time in which it is discovered that all illnesses, one way or another, come from the mind. For even an accident has to be caused by a distracted individual or someone who miscalculated some action. And that "distraction" or "miscalculation" does not originate in any other area of the body except the brain. As such, the way we communicate, react, interact and decide, is determined by the morons we associate with or encounter in our daily life. The more we expose ourselves to idiots and call them normal, the sicker we are likely to get.

A successful person is never successful alone but is certainly successful by the use of individual reasoning. The same applies to the one who manages to keep his own sanity. He must know the difference between what is normal and what is not.

It is when people start equalizing A, B and C, and saying that if A is friends to B, then C must be wrong, or that if one isn't A or B, then he is a C, because there is no such thing as D, that they truly set themselves to insanity.

We can certainly say that stupidity predeceases mental illness, although the opposite is also true. A person that is mentally ill is always stupid.

What can we then say about the criminal psychopaths and the cruel narcissists? Aren't they always smart?

Only if we would assume that being smart is considered to be an instinct of survival adapted to the environment.

In other words, the psychopath and the narcissist are very suited for their environment — the sick world in which we live. But if you move them to a healthy environment, they then will seem very dumb and unable.

How much can a narcissist do inside a group that has high moral values? How much can a psychopath do in an environment of people with high levels of empathy?

UNCOMMON: TRANSCENDING THE LIES OF THE MENTAL HEALTH INDUSTRY

You see, their actions and results are determined by the weaknesses of the individuals of our society. As long as we assume that being good is a weakness of character, psychopaths and narcissists will be having a lot of fun. It is when we start valuing kindness that they then become seen as how they really are — weak and very sick individuals.

Kindness and morality is indeed a strength of character. Religion teaches people to fake it. And the educational institutions teach people to pretend they have it through their social cover. As a matter of fact, education serves more as a mechanism of social indoctrination, rather than education.

People think schools teach. No! They don't! That was never their purpose. School train conformity, by forcing mass amounts of people to sit, shut up and obey authority. The rest is a puppet show wasting tax money.

The solution to this mass imbecility starts with questioning. But it's like going on a graveyard and shouting to wake up the dead.

Most people are braindead. They don't care, can't understand, and in most cases, won't listen.

Chapter 8: Why Are Most People Predictable?

When there's a reason to be depressed, like the death of a loved one, depression is normal as a moment of grief, but can be prolonged more than usual if we spend too much time in confined places, as well as when we stop ourselves from having those emotions, by taking drugs.

The mass escape from emotions then conditions the majority to accumulate and suppress mental problems that come to the surface more often and in the least expected moments.

The constant fear of the unknown and strangers, that seems to be increasing in the world, leading to more xenophobia and divisions in society, is a symptom of this mass schizophrenia. A schizophrenia originating from the elimination of the sense of identity. Because, you see, the more people want to be part of something that is broken, the more they themselves will have to be broken to feel accomplished in this goal.

One of the problems people face nowadays is related to the lack of answers to the question: "What is my life purpose?"

They don't know what their life purpose is because they want to fit in into a society designed to mold them and enslave them as pieces of a machinery.

How could they know the answer, or answers to such question, if it necessarily implies individualism? In fact, the reason why most people can't understand my answers to this question, is due to the fact that they want to comprehend an answer related to individualism from the perspective of not having individualism. That's like teaching about the sun in a planet that never had one.

In essence, a life purpose is what makes you happy, and it's relative, reason why many will say something like: "I don't know what makes me happy!"

That's even more interesting than studying depression, because if people knew what made them happy in the first place, they would be doing things that uplift them, spending time with those that share joy and, in doing so, end up far from ever feeling depressed or lost.

It is mathematically certain, that the one who positions himself in a seemingly equation of morons and imbeciles, will subtract any and all of his positive behaviors from you at the end, including promises made, and result to be a zero.

To keep an association with such individuals is then to subtract from yourself and become less than zero — for you will lose your willingness, self-awareness and self-respect in the process.

Taking into consideration that depression and most mental illnesses arise out of emotions, it is certain to assume we absorb such emotions from our environment and suppress them when not processing them consciously.

Depression is related to fear, anxiety, needs and problems, while happiness is related to meaningful purposes, positive emotions and actions towards solutions. Therefore, it is easy to see which side is the most visible in our society.

If society, as a whole, was more uplifting, we wouldn't see so many people easily succumbing to mental illness and even suicide. The number of people who commit suicide in the world has been increasing because the level of insanity in the world has been increasing as well.

Chapter 9: What is The Line Between Sanity and Insanity?

You can increase the levels of happiness in an individual, and with this process, his mental health as well, by giving him a chance to do something useful for others, like working or helping someone else.

When psychiatrists or psychologists force a person to sit down and talk about his or her life problems, his or her childhood, what results is an increase of a passive behavior that leads to even more depression. The individual then ends up developing codependency towards the therapist, which results in a a maximization of profit for this, but a minimization of self-awareness for the individual.

The one inside the cycle of codependency then develops the idea that he or she is being helped when that is often not the case. It is the codependency that gives such illusion. Because the therapist ends up directing the other person's life with his insights on what should or shouldn't be done.

Most of what the psychologists address in their sessions, may seem logic, but isn't always necessary. To say that the childhood experience is related to depression in adulthood, for example, is like saying that a table is related to a house.

Sure it is, but do we need to change the whole decoration of the house just because the color of the table doesn't match it?

No, we just need to buy another table or learn to appreciate the rest of the house, or even the fact that we have one.

Many individuals I've personally met, say they improve their life, and overall mental health, much more in one hour talking with me, than in months talking to a psychiatrist, and yet, they prefer to pay the psychiatrist, believe him, and follow his advice.

In a recent case, I said to a person I could help her handle her traumas through a specific therapeutic procedure, and her question was:

— "Have you ever helped someone like me before?"

What surprised me in this question wasn't the question itself, but the fact that she never asked it to any of her psychologists, that clearly failed in helping her.

We have been programmed to believe that a diploma and a college degree are more important than reality. The faith in the governmental institutions made people blind to the most obvious.

One day I met a teacher who asked me:

— "What qualifies you to teach Spanish if you're not a native speaker?"

Even though I could provide a list of reasons, my answer was simple:

— "I can speak it!"

She didn't agree with the answer and appeared to be very frustrated and angry. So I asked in return:

— "What makes you competent to teach engineering?"

— "I have a PhD", She said.

— "You have a piece of paper", I replied her.

She felt confused with my answer, and I continued:

— "Do you believe that such piece of paper qualifies you?"

She was still confused and didn't know what to answer.

The thing is, we live in a very insane world, validating papers and naming them as being money or diplomas, but it's all part of a shared illusion, as they prove nothing but what we want them to be.

Those that I've interviewed in job applications for several companies used to say:

UNCOMMON: TRANSCENDING THE LIES OF THE MENTAL HEALTH INDUSTRY

— "How can I be rejected if I have a Master's Degree?"

— "You have a paper, but no evidence that you can actually perform the task well!", I told them. And nearly none understood this answer.

When people are confronted with the answers they don't want to hear, they reject even the one speaking. And then they proceed, insisting on other job applications, using the same methods. Because to change implies too much for them.

We assume that adulthood is about being independent and capable of making one's decisions, but that only applies to those who have been properly raised and trained.

The vast majority, has assimilated so many lies, once they become adults, they are actually only grown up bodies with childlike thinking patterns. They didn't truly grow up!

They never rationalize their behavior. They never questioned the system. They don't believe in questioning any authority. As a matter of fact, if 99% of those that apply for a job didn't focus on their behavior, but instead on what they can actually do, they could behave as they would like and speak as they want, and still get the job. Instead, they are extremely careful with their words and how they dress, because they invest all their skills on the appearance.

Moreover, as I've noticed, it is easier to be a spy in many organizations, and lie to highly qualified individuals, than anyone could possibly imagine, because most people are programmed to follow only one route of thought when analyzing reality. This direction chosen is the paradigm of the biggest social lie and everything matching it.

Chapter 10: Why People Sometimes Prefer Lies to The Truth?

There are psychologists in nearly every school in the most modern societies and teaching centers around the world, but they have absolutely no significant results with their students. In fact, they often believe that students with bad results suffer from mental illnesses. Therefore, these children end up receiving drugs like Ritalin or Valium (a very heavy antidepressant).

Despite this, when working with many children, I was able to help them achieve results that everyone said couldn't ever be possible. People believed I was just being lucky. But lucky every single time? And lucky dozens of times?

This, I believe, can describe well how the world functions. People hold on to obsessive patterns and beliefs, and conduct their existence accordingly, never questioning the validity of their beliefs, not even when confronted with the facts. How could they? There are just too many liars in the world.

During my time in college, I was basically paying to be brainwashed with imbecility. Took me years to realize all those teachers were arrogant ignorant imbeciles. And yet, they continue, to this day, preaching their own nonsense to the masses. And no wonder they are arrogant.

You see, when you spread a big lie, that doesn't match anything else, not God, not reality, not even your own life, you have to continue on doing so, because that is all you have and who you are. Without it, you have nothing else. Reason why I deduct hell would be a wonderful place for such souls.

Those who spread lies to pull the world from moving forward, while in positions of power, are worse than evil spirits. They represent the most disgusting creatures one could imagine to exist. If our world is still stuck to lies, it is because it is contaminated with these parasites.

One's health could then automatically improve by simply developing the courage to look at the truth, to say: "That's a whole bunch of bullshit, and I won't take it anymore!"

The second stage of this process, is to seek for the right answers.

Most mental health experts say that admitting a problem is 50% of the process to achieve a cure. And I agree! Acknowledging that their science is rooted on lies, is 50% of anyones' cure. To believe that they can help anyone, rather than butchering the intellectual capacity of their patients, is to head towards 0% of the path towards a cure. And that's why most of such people never get cured from anything. They get a stamp for life related to their supposedly incapacities.

The reason why trusting lies moves one apart from the truth should be self-evident. But the facts are not within the reach of those who are unable to look at themselves. And that's why narcissism is such a widespread mental illness.

Narcissism is a very thick mask, when we can't face our problems, find the answers, or let anyone know that we suffer from the same problems they do. Because they won't acknowledge it, and for the same reasons.

We see this behavior even in situations where one would expect people to use reason. "When DNA evidence was conclusive, police and prosecutors often fought back to try to keep people behind bars. Rather than accepting the evidence and trying to reform their systems, they tried to protect their integrity.

This, in a way, makes sense: admitting you are wrong can call into question not just your skills or job, but your very vocation. When a prosecutor, who spent years at law school and climbed his way up the legal system, is exposed as presenting a case with huge holes in it, or convicted the wrong person who has spent years in jail, he may feel as if his whole career is a sham. No wonder evidence will be rejected, no matter how powerful or insurmountable" (Tom Butler Bowdon).

"DNA evidence is indeed strong, but not as strong as the desire to protect one's self-esteem" (Matthew Syed).

Chapter 11: Why Does Misinterpretation Happen?

Those who know more are often seen as knowing less, because they are different from what the majority, a stupid but arrogant majority, thinks.

In a highly insane world, the different ones are those that can actually survive to it. But why should anyone care? One person alone can't change the world!

It is then such a shocking surprise when we allow ourselves to sink under waters of illusion?

You see, that which you don't oppose, becomes you. "In the big lie there is always a certain force of credibility; because the broad masses, in the primitive simplicity of their minds, more readily fall victims to the big lie than the small lie, since they themselves often tell small lies in little matters but would be ashamed to resort to large-scale falsehoods. It would never come into their heads to fabricate colossal untruths, and they would not believe that others could have the impudence to distort the truth so infamously. Even though the facts which prove this to be so may be brought clearly to their minds, they will still doubt and waver and will continue to think that there may be some other explanation" (Adolf Hitler, In 'Mein Kampf').

When someone criticizes me for being different, thinking differently or doing things differently, for example, I actually see it as a compliment. It's because I am different that I am happier and more fulfilled than most people I've ever met.

I've been interviewed on radios, both European and North American, and done many other things that seem unbelievable, but I don't talk about it anymore because people can't understand the real purpose of what I share. They just hate and ask more questions for something they can't possibly accept. And so, I've came to the conclusion that in a world of zombies it is better to be invisible. It's not worth to fight back a crazy world.

Once you finally understand what happiness is, you will realize that you are alone. The majority of the world is sad, angry, anxious or frustrated. This is, by the way, what movies and TV series show us all the time and reason why many watch them.

However, when you choose to immerse yourself in the subconscious patterns of the masses, you choose to sell yourself to that ideal too — that self-projected intuitive falsehood that life is a competition and one can only win by defeating others.

"Nothing is more intimately our own than our character, which is determined by nothing other than our free and self-determined choices. And since evil is a privation, a kind of non-being or nothingness, the more one makes morally evil choices, the "less" one becomes. In other words, choosing moral evil, such as treating another or others as a means to an end, brings about a shrinkage, a lessening of the self.

If perpetuated and unrepented, such de-creation leads to a kind of self-loathing; for there is less of oneself to love just as the more one severs pieces of one's face with a knife, the more unsightly he becomes and the more horrified he is as he beholds his reflection in a mirror" (Douglas McManaman).

You can benefit a lot from putting your TV in the trash and never watch it again, because the TV is made for the majority and that majority is sick, and as such, Television is promoting sickness – violence, fear and hate.

Chapter 12: Why Losing Friends Can Be a Blessing?

When the truth becomes a widely spread lie, and the biggest lie is a common truth, then your only way is a rejection of everything that is accepted, and towards a path that gives you a happiness you may never be able to communicate effectively, because nobody will understand. "If each day you are unsure of who you are and what you know, you will never become anything, and that is your reward" (Oscar Wilde).

Wherever I go in the world, people say to me: "I wish I had your life!"

They will never have my life! You know why? Because they are too scared to be different, to develop their own individuality. Therefore, what they envy, they can't have.

Their envy is a projection of their cowardice. They want what I have by following the path of the lie. And that's why they will never have it. But they know no other path! So they will continue along that route, and then, every time they feel stupid, imbecile and incompetent, they'll fabricate a lie to justify my success and switch off the lights of their consciousness. That is why they say I am lucky, or that I steal my knowledge from others, and so on.

Have you noticed that the majority always hates that which they can't understand?

When I was in school, everyone thought I was an idiot. When I had the highest grades, even the teachers couldn't believe. They would sit next to me, and ignore the other students, trying to find my ultra-sophisticated method of cheating. Now that I am an adult, everyone thinks I am committing a crime, because they just can't believe I can be so free.

My only crime was to take the freedom they will never have, because they are slaves — slaves to the system they trust.

It is sad to swim alone in a long empty beach of white sand and warm waters in the Philippines. It is sad to be able to go every day to the beach in the south of Spain and work there. It is sad to have the freedom to travel to any country by choice, alone. And do you know why it is sad? Because you understand that everyone you ever known believes a lie so blindly, they rather hate you and suffer than to join you.

This is why many of my relationships did not work, or why many of my friendships had to end, and why I enjoy their lie as my truth.

They could choose not to be stupid. All they had to do was buy one of my ebooks, which cost less than their toilet paper, but contain more value than all the words they will hear during their pathetic and insignificant existence.

It's a simple act, to pick up a book and just read it. But they won't!

I write everything I know. Everyone that writes books, is writing what they know. That is why reading, or listening to audiobooks, is so important to one's own education.

My sadness for them is then more like a projection of myself, for my awareness brought me to the realization that I can only evolve on my own.

You can't force a donkey to be a horse. Not everyone was born to be an eagle, and enjoy life from the high skies of freedom. But that's what evolution is. If you are too comfortable with slavery and darkness, you are not evolved enough.

Chapter 13: What Does it Mean to Lack Empathy?

It can be noticed in blogs originating from different parts of the world, that there are many individuals saying that they would take prozac even while knowing its risks, because, according to such individuals, if even rats are willing to eat rat poison, there must be something good or right in it.

Others say that, if prozac is so popular and famous, there must be some positive effects in it.

When some of my students researched this phenomenon, they decided to create specific forums to chat with people about it, and understand their motivations. And they were shocked to notice that most people systematically create justifications for all the evils that were done unto them, in order to deny the seriousness of the facts.

It is said that a lie repeated times enough becomes a common truth. And if psychologists keep comparing human beings with rats, people will eventually believe they are just rats. This can also be seen as mass hypnosis.

If you are a professional hypnotist with a scientific paper backing you up, you can even make people believe they are pigs, donkeys and chickens. There is just no evidence that they will put eggs after that, just like there's no evidence that prozac is good for mental health.

Now, with these facts in mind, you can take responsibility for your life while allowing others to take responsibility for their death. Because, you see, most people live absorbed in their own mind and routines, in a kind of numb state of living, reminding us of what can be seen in movies about zombies.

This commonality may very well explain the popularity of these movies in recent times, as well as the rising cases of individuals that murder others to eat them, or that bite other people.

Even if, in all registered cases, drugs prescribed were the reason behind what occurred, the label of "insane" is still being used as the main explanation, and not "drugged with dangerous psychotropics".

What can we actually do about it? In our childhood we obey teachers to pass exams and our parents not to be grounded, or beaten in some cases, and when we become adults, we obey to keep a job. There is not much we can do about our life that wouldn't be seen as a radical decision by others.

Nevertheless, the best defense against psychological aggression is empirical analysis. You must be able to analyze the meaning behind the concepts used against you to know that they're usually made to keep you ignorant.

Now, when a vast portion of society is under some form of psychotropic drug, the probability of encountering someone who is not very able is high. Such people tend to be more afraid of the world around them, and get dominated by their instincts. Therefore, they may be very aggressive when things don't go their way.

Most of the insults that people say to each other are actually projections of their own subconscious mind, and not related to the person in front of them. If you can focus on the reasons behind any insult, you may notice this, and then the words have less effect on you. The more analytical you can be about the whole situation, the less you will feel like a victim. And the same applies to anything else that you have to deal with in your life.

Increasing your capacity to analyze the problems does distance you from such problems. It is our emotions that pull us in and absorb us, many times, inside events that occurred years ago, and we can't seem to forget.

Writing about our problems can also help in analyzing our experiences, and by expressing our confusions, fears and depression, we can actually develop the necessary ability to have a good cognitive awareness and processing of our thinking patterns.

The same will happen when we talk to someone about our issues.

UNCOMMON: TRANSCENDING THE LIES OF THE MENTAL HEALTH INDUSTRY

To a great extent, the increasing of mental illnesses is also related to a decreasing sharing and socializing in our world as a whole. People are more individualistic, superficial and less given to sharing their life with others. And this has certainly an effect on their mental health.

We need our friends, family and intimate relationship to be a pillar of strength in our self-esteem. But that rarely happens now. Most people have high expectations on us, and too many fears to respect our personal will. They end up wanting to destroy our life for their own good.

If you talk about your personal love life with others, for example, this becomes pretty obvious. Few if any people, can truly listen to you empathically. The empathy levels have been decreasing tremendously.

Chapter 14: What is Metacognitive Therapy?

It has been found that the only therapies in psychology that show significant results, are either metacognitive based therapies or group therapies. In both cases, people are expressing what they feel, so that they can analyze themselves and their choices better.

These techniques work because they help in rehabilitating the capacity to understand our own personal problems. This is also the reason why art has such positive effects on our well-being.

Those who help children with learning disabilities using art — music, drawing, painting, sculpture and so on — are following exactly the same principles, and they work every single time, making the students smarter and reach better grades in any given topic, with any teacher. As a result, we can say that expressing emotions develops our cognitive ability and overall mental health. As a matter of fact, I've never met a person that plays a musical instrument and is dumb or even slightly insane, or that has bad school grades because he or she can't learn.

We may find mentally ill individuals believing they can be musicians but that's another story and their lack of success has more to do with their mind than their "hidden talent".

It has become obvious, from my own personal experience in music, that the only way to make a musician develop a tendency for depression and apathy, consists in leading him to drugs of any kind. Moreover, the best DJs and music producers I have encountered in my life were artists, engineers and teachers, that very often used these musical activities as a way to relieve stress from their daily work.

With these facts in hand, you can take responsibility for your intelligence and lifestyle while allowing others to take responsibility for their ignorance. Because, you see, you may have to develop two very different cycles in your existence, in order to keep your mental integrity. And hopefully, that second cycle is not a destructive addiction, as what happens with the vast majority of the people, but a healthy one.

Playing sports in groups you can identify with, managing a part-time business, even if not lucrative for the first years, developing a hobby related to art, or just reading, are crucial for balancing our mind with the pressure coming from our environment.

Two of the most famous movies that represent our options in life are 'Forrest Gump' and 'Life of Pi'. Forrest Gump, teaches us that if we keep running, we will eventually get somewhere in life, even if all the probabilities and facts are against us. There is actually a biblical quote that says the same: "Run in such a way that you may win" (Corinthians 9:24). This is a quote about persistence and about never giving up. The same teaching presented by the movie 'Life of Pi'.

You understand in 'Life of Pie', that life is like a boat inside a storm: You can either sink with the rest of the people, or survive on your own, which may lead you to dangerous adventures, having to face many and constant dangers on your own.

Either way, a path will eventually be made out of nothing and nowhere. The only thing you need to fear is your own fears. Which in 'Life of Pie' is symbolized by the tiger.

Life doesn't change when we get older. It becomes worse. But there are always small islands waiting for us in every unexpected place. And, at that point, life becomes about finding those islands, rather than escaping danger. The islands are our moments of happiness, the places that uplift us, the people that make us smile.

Those who can find their happiness, learn soon to take the highest risks and keep moving forward, because they understand that life is about that happiness.

UNCOMMON: TRANSCENDING THE LIES OF THE MENTAL HEALTH INDUSTRY

In the movie 'Rocky', a memorable conversation between father and son, shows us exactly this wisdom, when the father says: "The world ain't all sunshine and rainbows. It is a very mean and nasty place and I don't care how tough you are, it will beat you to your knees and keep you there permanently if you let it. You, me, or nobody is gonna hit as hard as life. But it ain't about how hard you hit; it's about how hard you can get hit, and keep moving forward. It's about how much you can take, and keep moving forward. That's how winning is done. Now, if you know what you're worth, then go out and get what you're worth. But you gotta be willing to take the hits, and not point fingers and blame other people. Cowards do that and that ain't you. You're better than that!"

Every good movies must resemble facts. And indeed, what makes the 'Life of Pi' particularly interesting is that the movie director had to wash dishes in the United States for years before having the opportunity to prove his value in the movie industry. As for Sylvester Stallone, the writer and actor in 'Rocky', he wrote this movie when starving, without a place to live or a job, and after having to sell his own dog to pay for food. Many movie directors told him that he couldn't be the actor of his own movie, because he was not a good actor. To fulfill his dream, even when the odds where against him, Stallone rejected every profitable proposal received, and ended up accepting one that paid him a very small amount of money.

He accepted that small offer, bought his dog back, put his dog in the first movie of 'Rocky', and ended up, not only filming one of the most successful and inspiring movies we have ever seen, but also making himself one of the most popular and well-paid movie Actors.

Not less difficult was the life of another actor, named Arnold Schwarzenegger. An emigrant from a poor family in Austria that could't even talk proper English, and ended up being one of the most famous actors in the world, as well as the Governor of California.

Chapter 15: Why You Should Never Stop Loving Yourself?

Despite the fact that most people are not even slightly aware of how difficult was my past, I too came a long way to be where I am now.

I now make quite enough money to live a comfortable life and travel the entire world, when I want and where I want. But nobody prepared me for this, or helped me. On the contrary! I was told, during all of my years of school, and even up to college, that my writing was horrible.

The first time I talked to a psychologist, who happened to be also the school counselor, she told me I was a bit too retarded to go to University, and should instead try to find a simple job, related to merely carrying on simple tasks. She said being a security guard could be an option for me. And I wasn't born in the United States, but in a poor European country.

I spent most of my life trying to have enough money to pay for rent and food, and not end up in the streets. And yet, I did, when my parents divorced and none wanted me with them.

Later, I had to starve myself in order to have enough money to pay for a small flat. The many jobs I kept finding where very badly paid, and barely enough to survive.

For nearly all of my life, up until I was 30yo, I had no hope, no dreams, no opportunities, nothing. All I had were several people waiting for me to commit suicide.

Then, one after another, miracles happened. They came in the form of new job opportunities abroad, new friendships and new relationships.

When the time came to make a very difficult decision — to choose between my dream, with a very high probability of failure, or the job of being a University Lecturer, and everything else, like a rich girlfriend who wanted to marry me but did not want me to be a poor writer, and the opportunity to move with her to the United States, and even join other business partner, most of whom had been students of mine, I did the unthinkable. I moved to Spain, and spent two years in a complete solitude. I lived in front of the beach but never swam in the ocean. I was always working, from morning to night. The time-limit was my savings. Once they runout, I would have nothing. No job, no wife, no money, nothing. I had burned all my ships!

I was suffering! But I was determined to either live a meaningful life or die trying.

When I was about to lose it all, including the house I was renting, my income as an author started increasing, and kept increasing ever since.

Today, I can tell you that many of my books have reached the number one position on the Amazon bestselling charts. I am one of the most sought self-help authors in the world. Not only with this author name you see here, but many other pen-names I created ever since. Yes, all of my pen-names, in different genres — self-help, religion, education, business, and psychology — became extremely popular.

That loser that everyone ignored, abandoned and thought that would end up living in the streets or committing suicide, that moron that could not even have a meaningful job, or write properly, according to everyone, including college professors, is now living a life most can only dream.

Surely, I don't recommend anyone to try and become a full-time writer. In this field, you either succeed as the top 0,1% or you burn like the other 99.9%. There isn't a worse career to choose from, with the lowest probability of success. I resumed here a huge amount of challenges that I have faced. But what I want to tell you is that people insult me whenever they call me lucky. They are too stupid, too unaware, too faraway from ever realizing how, literally impossible, it is to get what I have now, and how much I had to do to get where I am now. Some even think that I am possessed by demons or take heavy drugs, or sell drugs.

UNCOMMON: TRANSCENDING THE LIES OF THE MENTAL HEALTH INDUSTRY

Surely, when someone goes so far, you have to assume this person did something drastic, as selling his soul, sell drugs or take drugs. They just can't accept the truth! But I never took drugs, I never even smoked and I don't drink alcohol. I don't eat meat. I'm a vegan. I never sold drugs. And I never sold my soul to the devil. But I have been attacked by demons, and quite a lot, during the moments I was writing the most important books. Not even priests wanted to help me! Yeah, fuck them all too! I had to help myself, and read about exorcism and different types of prayer to keep moving on.

That's how much I had to fight to be where I am now! I battled both the physical world and the spiritual world! I battled both in my mind, and my emotions, and the people I cared about and tried to stop me. And that is why there is such an energy in my books.

Some, too dumb to see it, will simply assume I am an angry person. There is certainly anger when you are so immensely betrayed by so many people. But that's an underestimation of what I am doing. And yet, here I am, revealing everything I know to you.

When you apply what I tell you, you don't just succeed in whatsoever is the title of what I write, but everything else too. If I was able to fight and win against a whole world, just imagine what you can do in anything else! It is only natural and expectable, that everyone that learns from me becomes far more successful than I am. That is actually often the case! I have to live with the fact that most of my dedicated followers are extremely rich and far much more than me.

We all die one day, but not many people actually live. But life is not about what you have. It is about what you believe. Life is a choice that can only be rejected. So embrace life and love yourself, always, and under any circumstance!

Chapter 16: How to Attract More Opportunities in Your Life?

In the field of mental health there's something called the "point of no return", when an individual can't be helped anymore, and there isn't any therapy, physical or psychological, able to provide a healing.

Interestingly, this situation includes mainly victims of lobotomy, electroconvulsive therapy and psychotropics, while modern medicine commonly labels patients in such a state, most of which suffering with cancer or other dangerous diseases, as "terminal".

However, a situation can't be that bad before reaching what can be defined as a path of choices and decisions. For everything that happens to us can be reversible.

Everyone chooses to live or to die, to pursue dreams or embrace nightmares, to accept love or indulge in self-destructive behaviors. Every prayer, dream, and belief, opens doors for possibilities and opportunities that come to our life in many ways. Nothing is as bad as a lack of hope.

On the other hand, we must be aware that drugs used in psychiatry do more arm than good. Such drugs suppress human emotions and repress self-acknowledgment.

The point of no return, then starts when the individual gives away his own right to be responsible for his fate or is somehow forced to do so.

In order to know how to cure a mental illness we must necessarily analyze our personal choices and the lack of them, so that we may find a path for rehabilitation before it is too late.

There is something common in everyone suffering from a mental illness, and it is the fact that somewhere in the past of that person, something happened, leading to such state. But we don't suffer from what happens as much as we suffer from what we do to ourselves after that. Most people suffering from depression have gone that way through self-destructive attitudes, such as selfishness, greediness, perversion, promiscuity and evilness.

Even though these personality traits may be stimulated by the suffering endured in many moments of our life, they are the real reason behind a perpetual suffering.

The impossibility to change the past and take revenge is more poisonous to the mind than any incident. Because we then go in cycles within our mind from which we can't seem to detach. And isn't that why people seek for the therapist? So that they can detach?

Instead, when receiving the prescription for a psychotropic drug, they repress the problem. And if the psychologist is incompetent, and many are, this person may never truly analyze the problem effectively.

Most psychologists turn victims of domestic abuse into whores, and women who are incapable to love into drug addicts. They do this because they are too stupid to give advice to anyone.

Quite often, personal mentors and coaches do more for people than therapists. Because you can say that someone is a victim of biology or unfortunate life experiences, but it doesn't change the fact that you may have two real cases of individuals growing in very violent environments, in which one became a professional fighter and the other ends in jail for smuggling cocaine. One becomes a professional boxer and the other is just another number in some cell of the United States. Both of which may have been raised in the same neighborhood.

In other two cases of individuals suffering from depression, one may became a writer and the other part of the statistics on suicide. And both may have been colleagues and friends in university, as was the case between me and a friend I met in college.

UNCOMMON: TRANSCENDING THE LIES OF THE MENTAL HEALTH INDUSTRY

Finally, between two individuals suffering from anxiety and depression due to unemployment, one may take chances abroad and became a professor in a University, while the other ends up as a patient in some mental hospital. And again, this was also part of my background, as such was the fate of two of my friends.

You see, it is never about the challenges we face as much as it is about our willingness to get more from life — our attitude to life.

I've never met an altruistic person, who was not willing to voluntarily help others, suffering from depression. When you show compassion for others, that may be enough to open your heart to receive love in return, at least in the form of a smile. And it will be enough to reinforce your self-esteem and self-belief, and open you for new possibilities.

Those who believe that everything in life is about personal gain and the accumulation of money, become a black hole where nothing is ever enough. Eventually, they push love out of their lives by not noticing what they already have and appreciating it.

What you get is determined by your potential value, and your value as an individual is determined by your level of faith and hope, towards others, yourself and life as a whole. If you expect nothing, want nothing and don't believe in anything, you are as good as dead. You are a useless being to yourself, to others and to the planet. And so, we can very well say that, while some go through life living like suns, others are like black holes, sucking the life of everyone else, their own energy, resources and emotions.

What I just said is actually a simple fact that seems somehow invisible to many, even tabu and rejected by the majority of society. But the majority has always been too stupid anyway. The stupid solutions found in the realms of science and medicine shows us exactly that.

In a normal world, everything that we see on this planet would seem ridicule, absurd and even barbaric. But when a people are too stupid, they call what I just said normal. And yet, whenever you normalize yourself to the level of your environment, you become a well-adapted moron.

The solution to many problems then consists on living above the standards. Most seek this financially, but never consider the same through their own sanity and intelligence. They want to be rich, while stupid and insane. And even though such is indeed a possibility, it merely represents another step sideways rather than upwards.

Moving upwards typically means being perfectly aware that most people you know may never understand you. And that's fine! A little piece of heaven is always better than a vast amount of hell.

What I am trying to tell you is that it is better to shine alone than to live in darkness with others.

Chapter 17: What is The True Meaning of Evil?

There is always a choice in following evil deeds or not. When we talk about Karma, Law of Attraction, Eye for an Eye, The Golden Rule, or any other similar law that is known to many, we're referring to the same thing: What goes around comes around.

Whatsoever we choose and for whatever reason, is a personal choice, even though many claim that they were persuaded into doing their actions somehow.

"He made me do it", is something that even the nazis answered when questioned about their crimes.

Now, what is truly interesting here, is that even the narcissists, known for the most calculated acts of evil, tend to blame their own victims and say the same: "He made me do it."

This said, it is important to notice that our environments conditions us towards certain types of experiences, either as an aggressor or as a victim. Reason why experts know that nobody dies alone in a suicide. Many conversations and exchanges of motivations and emotions have occurred before that incident. We could go from here to say that nobody gets mentally ill alone, depressed alone or unsuccessful in life alone, and that is actually true to a great extent too.

The media and society in general lead everyone to believe that certain values, behaviors and beliefs, which should be avoided, are to be followed. And so, aggression now, even though not so much used through weapons, still occurs with words. Most people are not stabbed with knifes and swords, but words. And is this less bad? I'm not sure on how to answer you, if we consider how debilitating depression can be.

Let us go from here and ask ourselves: Is the person that steals money more evil than the one who deliberately allows us to lose it?

The world is designed to steal, to attack, and to murder. The ways are simply more subtle now. Which means that our connections are much more important than before, as we can't trust anyone as easily as centuries ago. And is the person who pretends a friendship more friendly than the one refusing it?

I would say that, under uncertainty, I choose to reject friendships. I have no regrets, even though I have lost many thousands of friends over the years, most of which came from the many popular activities I had.

When you are famous, either as a President of a University, a spokesperson, a business manager, a musician, and so on, everyone wants to be your friend and tell others they know you.

With writers as well, even though authors don't have the same social impact DJs do, and so, it is not so common in this case. Most of the people who want my friendship now are typically other authors trying to get some information from me on how to force their shitty books on the market and profit without any value, just to get their ego stroke.

Being famous, however, doesn't grant you better friends. Just more bullshit! You have more people pretending to be something they're not, just to get close to you.

I have learned, through the course of my existence, that if I want to keep my mental sanity, and not do something dumb, like punch someone in the face — and many do deserve it — and ruin my reputation because of some imbecile that lacks childlike attention, I need to be very careful with the type of people I allow to enter my life. And that is why even though they enter quickly, they are quickly removed too.

We may have heard often that is not correct to judge others, and yet, we are judged by what we do and say all the time. But there is actually no need to judge others, if you let them judge themselves.

UNCOMMON: TRANSCENDING THE LIES OF THE MENTAL HEALTH INDUSTRY

It's very simple to do that! As I always said to my students, who asked me to evaluate their personality and decisions in life, "Judge not yourself or others, except when you are being judged, and then judge those who judged you instead and by how they judged."

You see, many people say more about themselves when talking about you, and so, if you really want to understand yourself, and correct your actions or thoughts, it is better to observe them doing such self-projections. Because then you can judge yourself by judging them.

Our world is a gigantic labyrinth of mirrors. You think you are walking through life and facing different experiences, while in fact you keep encountering experiences that mirror you and others, but others in particular when they want to judge you.

Judgement is an act of analysis and no analysis can be done without a significant amount of self-reflection.

Because most people don't introspect, they don't even listen themselves speaking when talking about others. They regurgitate their own fears, insecurities and beliefs the whole time.

Chapter 18: Why Do We Need Introspection?

Two thousand years have passed but I don't think this world has understood the main message in the story of Jesus Christ, either you choose to believe that he was real or fiction, either you choose to believe he walked on water and resurrected, or not.

That's not the point! You have to invert the whole context and use it to mirror yourself and the world that surrounds you. And then, but only then, you will see that nothing changed. We still have religious intolerance, we still have a mass misinterpretation of religious texts, we still have arrogance in the priesthood of many sects, and hypocrisy in the hearts and minds of the many religious leaders.

The Vatican, through its banking system and massive amounts of gold and hidden scripture, has gone far beyond what could have merely infuriated Christ when he was alive. And many, truly many people, are still excluded from various temples, for whatsoever reason attributed to their character, personality or past. You are still insulted and rejected for asking the right questions, and falsely accused and disrespected for, quite frankly, doing what Jesus did, and that led him to his death — show the mistakes of the liars.

The world is still full of morons! Their behavior is the same as it was! They can't beat you and crucify you for doing these things, but they surely would if they could. The widespread study of christianity changed nothing. The cult of schizophrenia, often named as religion, perfectly justifies atheism. But atheism is quite simply the only answer to a world that ignores the need to ask the right questions or answer them.

Most christians and other cult members don't like the idea that they may very well be nothing more than a schizophrenic cult or that the God they pray to is actually Lucifer. And the group in itself, protects them from such introspection, as if a shared lie became truth by default. And yet, a lie doesn't become truth because of faith.

The whole purpose of faith is not to become a happy lunatic. Although, quite sadly, even those who follow the path of the psychotropics, end up in the same trap, when trusting science as if it was a religion.

Much has yet to be learned. These two thousand years brought little to mankind. Evolution, on a personal or planetary level, then requires the same type of introspection as a therapeutic procedure. But how can you introspect in this lunatic house called earth? How can you expect your therapist, who is a perfectly fit member of the system, to help you?

This awareness leads you to the only path that shows you salvation, and it's not religion or psychiatry or medicine, or any form of drugs, but quite simply self-love.

Chapter 19: What Are The Benefits of Self-Love?

Loving ourselves demands difficult choices in life but, when someone chooses to contribute to our unhappiness, that person made his or her choice clearly already, whoever he or she is, whatever past is shared, and for whatsoever reason is presented as an excuse.

When we take advices from others, we make a choice! When hating out of gossips and stories, we make a choice too! And we are responsible for all the choices we make, as well as their consequences.

Even though a large part of the world population is not wise enough to make proper choices in life, reason why only a few command the rest, there's always the option to feel accomplished for the many things we have done, namely, by being independent in life and enjoying things that others wish they had.

Consciousness should be the main guidance behind our actions, and compassion the ultimate judge of them. But if we can't do that, we can, at the very least, focus on improving ourselves while not hurting others.

There are many ways to hurt and diminish others, and we tend to do that by transferring the same behavior that others once applied on us. Reason why those who hurt tend to show little or no compassion for their victims. They have learned their behavior and it makes them feel superior to others, while when they were victims of the same behavior they were portraying the role that they want now to impose on others.

To a great extent, most people end up representing roles in society, and not really living their life. They are stuck in their past, recreating the same dramas.

You can see this in a variety of ways.

To say to a person that he doesn't look like what he wants to become, for example, is a form of diminishing that person. To distort the intentions of others, assuming they're evil, such as by saying, "You helped me because you want something from me", is a form of nullifying their good intention.

The opposite is surely something very hardly seen in our modern world, namely, the supporting of others, with words and inspiring compliments.

You can do a lot more for those in depression and yourself, even while under such state, by sharing motivational quotes, such as "Never let your memories be greater than your dreams" (Doug Ivester) because "The only limit to our realization of tomorrow will be our doubts of today" (Franklin Delano Roosevelt).

"An individual must rise above an avid craving for agreement from a humanoid group to get anything decent done" (L. Ron Hubbard). And the positive messages you repeat to yourself and the ones you care about must be more louder and more effective than the negative messages you and them hear from others.

Chapter 20: How to Stop Running Away From Yourself?

In most cases, our mental illnesses can be solved based on a simple principle: Confront and forget!

The path, however, still requires plenty of work from the scientific community. Although, one way or another, all therapies tend to go in the same direction. The question, I would say, is in how to confront and how to forget.

In essence, to confront means dealing with a problem without giving any emotion to it, to just look at those who criticize us, insult us and end up acting as disgusting human beings, without putting any emotion into the interaction. Because, we also attract that which we experience. Hatred attracts hatred, disappointment attracts disappointment and frustration leads to more frustration.

On the other hand, when constantly attracting the same type of problems, we must ask ourselves why is this constantly occurring. And I'm not talking about guilt but rather responsibility.

The difference is this: guilt tells you that you must endure the situation. Responsibility says that there is something you must learn about yourself in other to change the outcome.

Changing a situation doesn't mean to accept it and tolerate it, but rather overcome it.

For example, if I realize that meat isn't good for my health, I change my diet to solve the problem. Likewise, if a certain city doesn't welcome me, there's no point in confronting the locals for imbecility or racism. It is better to leave and forget all that.

This principle applies to anything else. If your problems have a specific cause, not being the effect of that cause is the starting point to solve them.

That may require you to change job or even country. There's nothing wrong with those changes.

What can we then understand about ourselves, when we change environment and face the same type of experiences?

Well, as an example, if we keep attracting bosses that are aggressive and disrespectful , it means that we don't respect ourselves. If our spouse doesn't respect us, the same applies. If we are constantly being betrayed and cheated by different people, it simply means we don't value ourselves enough, and this is why certain personalities enter our life. It is not about them as much as it is about us.

As soon as I started raising my self-esteem, my bad relationships with narcissists went from lasting years, to lasting only a few weeks.

Now, most narcissistic women don't even want to talk to me. My whole energy repels them. They are attracted to me, to my empathic behavior and achievements, but as soon as they realize I am into them, they vanish like ghosts in the night.

I could look at these situations and think: "It' seems I can't keep a woman around!"

In fact, I can. But not the ones I want. And this, I would say, is my next stage in the healing process.

I know what I want. All I need to do is keep rejecting what I do not want.

What does a narcissist not want? An empath that doesn't tolerate their bullshit.

What does an empath want? Another empath, or at least someone who doesn't act like a narcissist.

One of the things I have noticed in the past six months, by dating seven different women, is that a large portion of them is broken. And as much as men are broken.

UNCOMMON: TRANSCENDING THE LIES OF THE MENTAL HEALTH INDUSTRY

It's difficult for me to even make friends with men. But in what regards women, many have experienced too much trauma to be able to look at a relationship in a healthy way.

As I grow older, it is difficult for me to tolerate someone that wants to end the peace of mind that I worked very hard to have.

My life is great! I can travel when I want and go where I want. I can write books when I want, or not, if I don't want. I can spend an entire month producing music if that is what I want. And so, I can say I am totally in love with my life.

Someone else entering it would have to complement all this. And that is often not the case.

Because of the need for validation, most people judge too much and too wrongly. They don't know anything about life or money, and insist too much on topics that they were brainwashed to believe. And their own stupidity is not my responsibility. Even though the gap between most people and me is now too wide for me to also fulfill my emotional goals.

I am, at the very least, aware of the challenges and steps needed to overcome. And that is quite important, when introspecting ourselves, so that we don't fall into the mistakes of others.

Most people are so obsessed with cycles of self-destruction, that they don't even know they are in one.

Chapter 21: How to Overcome The Illusion of Fear?

Our attachments keep us within certain mental paradigms, and fear is what keeps those attachments alive. As soon as you stop conforming to the regulations of others or accepting their lack of respect, most will vanish from your life. And that's fine! What is not fine, is when you want to fit in so badly, that you allow others to step on your self-esteem.

Fear is the root of all evil, but evil has as much power as we allow it to have. If we succumb to our fears, such as the fear of losing a job, the fear of losing a spouse, and even the fear of dying, then those fears will feed on our soul, starting with our awareness, thoughts and emotions.

Fear is a poison! If we allow this poison to consume us, we may never know how we went from one point to another, and then another, ending up in a whole mountain of problems.

Whenever someone describes me her problems, this becomes quite evident, reason why sometimes it's hard to be supportive of someone that comes our way.

For example, a woman once complained to me that the father of her daughter was very evil and was constantly giving her problems. From her description, it seemed to me that this man was motivated by opportunity. And so, I asked her:

— Did you sleep with him after the divorce.

She said: — Yes.

And then I asked: — Why did you have a baby with him?

She was too dumbfound to answer this last question. But the main point is this: She chose him, she chose to sleep with him after he beat her enough to fill her face full of bruises, and multiple times, and she was still meeting with him, for whatever reason.

She didn't like my questions, so my relationship with her ended soon after.

She actually asked me to help her solve this problem. But how? By killing the guy?

She created this problem and fed it with sex for nearly ten years. She even had a daughter with him. So what did she do with her psychiatrist? I'm not sure, as that therapist was clearly a total waste of money.

You see, in some cases we must ask why do people like their dramas so very much. And also if they get a mental illness or predispose themselves to have one. Can it be related to fear? Or the addiction to the fear?

The main point is this: If you allow a problem to persist, that problem becomes you, and then you are the problem you tried to escape from. In other words, she lost me, not because I did not help her, but because she refused to help herself when she decided to disappear from my life.

Apparently, she thinks that her dumb friends are more useful, when getting drunk with her to hear about her problems, and the many guys who entered her life weren't qualified.

The truth is what people want it to be. If they choose to believe that their life can't be changed, then they won't ever change it. It's as simple as that!

In this story that I just told you, she didn't realize that I could simply remove her from that country and help both her and her daughter restart a new life. Her fears controlled her mind, and she remained where she was.

People often complain of lack of opportunities, but from what I have noticed, most of the times, they do have the opportunities. They just don't realize it. They insist on remaining on the same place, attached to routines and people, until those people vanish, to pursue their own goals, the routines change, and nothing is left for them.

In order to overcome the illusions and the challenges, you do need to go beyond them, and not let go of the opportunities that come your way.

UNCOMMON: TRANSCENDING THE LIES OF THE MENTAL HEALTH INDUSTRY

Paying the price is part of it, but in time, any sacrifice is worth it.

Do I regret the sacrifices I made to get where I am now? If I did, I wouldn't be where I am.

The only thing I regret is not being more focused and determined. I regret doubting myself often and not having more self-discipline.

Basically, I would have done the same if going back in time, but I do regret not having done it all much faster and with less self-pity.

Chapter 22: Why are People Afraid of Change?

Nobody suffers alone, and nobody fails or succeeds alone either. You can even guess the personality of someone by analyzing his closest friends. And you can also presume his main difficulties ahead of time by doing the same.

As a matter of fact, we tend to attract the most, people who reflect both our desires and fears. We should never judge them before looking within ourselves.

Now, the subconscious fear that many have in regards to changing the personality, is related to that knowing, that once something in them shifts, the outside world will change as well, and they will then lose the attachments they once had. That means losing friendships, as not everyone will support our changes.

People tend to make a certain image of who we are in their mind, and when we don't conform to that image, they feel uncomfortable, since everything they plan and think is related.

Changing is, nonetheless, part of life, and we do change for better or worse. Holding on to fears, however, is what makes us change negatively, because then life will force us into certain paths and experiences by default.

This said, we must be aware that, all the psychological elements have a spiritual component to them. Knowing how to confront a problem is also about learning how to deal with it in regards to the changes necessary for our personality, and this, in the alchemical fire of ascension.

That alchemical fire is shown in our emotions, namely, our anxieties and fears.

A smooth and natural transition in our life, should not have that but rather be accepted with joy. That joy must be the same when we decide to move to a new city, as when we are about to die. The excitement should be the same in both cases.

The great warriors of the past saw a great excitement in dying for a good cause, in a war for freedom. Because they were conditioned to see as valuable to fight for that which they believed.

In today's world people have little values and don't understand anymore the meaning of sacrificing one's life for a greater ideal. But either that ideal is a war for freedom, a financial goal you may have, or quite simply, finding the ideal country, the ideal city and the ideal spouse, the attitude behind it should be the same.

As you probably have noticed, it is actually difficult to divide our emotional investment in different areas of life. We tend to be the same in all areas. For many areas of my life, for example, I believed I could kept the waters divided — relationships, work and physical health. But as soon as I lost one relationship after another in only within weeks, with women I wanted to build a family with, and then saw myself getting fat, for working too much, I realized that would never happened. The more I invested in my work, to forget everything else, the more depressed and unhealthy I felt. Which led to me stopping everything entirely.

I may be very determined but I can't break the rules that govern our life. These laws follow a specific cycle that must be respected if we wish to evolve. In other words, I must take care of my health to increase my energy, and then work within a system of rules that allows me to socialize with others, and respect their limitations. Then, within that balance, I shall find the true joy, even if such joy comes with continuous challenges of a different nature, quite often related to the nature of others.

The difference in this case, I would say, consists in being responsible for your social life and how it affects you, rather than being a victim of random events. And certainly, as more and more people get out of control, fail and enter downward cycles, the more challenging it is to keep our environment at a certain level. But we do need all of those components to build our shield towards the fires of transmutation, without which we burn into abasement, apathy and sadness.

UNCOMMON: TRANSCENDING THE LIES OF THE MENTAL HEALTH INDUSTRY

Nobody faces greatest challenges than the one who is fighting for something that most do not want, and for that reason, nobody needs his friends, health and family more than such person.

Chapter 23: How Do You Focus on Solutions Rather Than Problems?

The vast majority of mental therapies out there won't teach you to confront your fears, and that's why they fail dramatically, even though the patient and his supposedly non-curable disease may be to blame for the lack of results.

Overcoming an issue doesn't mean deliberately erasing it from our memory or pretend it isn't happening through psychotropics. It means shifting our focus to something else, of a higher importance.

It is here that electroconvulsive therapy shows itself to be very dangerous, for it does neither one thing or the other, but rather deprives the patient from controlling his own perspective of reality with a random and unpredictable shift of focus forced by electroshocks.

That is atrocious and barbaric to the least!

A person who feels depressed should spend more time doing things that make him or her feel happy with life or just change life itself. In primitive times, people did not wondered in the same place, or with people they didn't like, being succumbed by their fears and problems. They just moved on to where life was more pleasant.

The concept can be translated to modern times as "solve it or leave it".

Following the same premise, insanity in the modern world can be resumed to a certain level of impotence in dealing with problems or even confronting them.

Another advantage of a deliberate change of focus, is that it matches what the quantum physicians describe as a quantum jump. For energy always follows our attention, and therefore, a transition must be followed by a shift of attention.

Quite often, our life begins to change once we shift our attention to something that is more uplifting for us. Which means that we don't necessarily even need to try to solve a problem without first moving forward to something else.

That is the main reason as to why therapists know that hobbies produce results in their patients. It's not the hobby in itself but the shift of attention that provides space for the mind to rehabilitate itself, and then operate more efficiently.

I remember, for example, that in the worse moment of my life, when I had no money or place to sleep, it was the shift of attention, towards music, martial arts, and associations in which I volunteered, that allowed me to think outside of that box, and eventually come with unthinkable solutions.

I was determined to succeed and the mistakes I did wouldn't stop me. But mistakes are not always within our control. The people that we expect to help us, don't, the friends in whom we trust betray us, and even our relatives turn their back on us.

Being betrayed is so part of my life, I am surprised whenever it doesn't happen. I actually thought it was a cultural thing, until I traveled the world and met people from many nations, and realized that almost everyone betrays.

Most people are selfish, self-centered and short-minded. Their main interest in life is themselves and everything or anything that surrounds them.

I have actually conducted some experiences of my own, to see how stupid people are, and realized they are truly very stupid. I have helped guys get girlfriends, I have helped people without hope, start a business of their own, and I have also offered quite a lot of secret knowledge, that the ones receiving didn't even know to exist, for free and voluntarily. I have offered free therapy to people who suffer from certain mental illnesses for years. I have helped women lose weight. I have helped students with serious learning difficulties achieve good grades. I have solved speech inabilities in autist children. And I am not christ, I don't perform miracles, but I have used my knowledge and unique abilities to the extent of what many consider impossible. And none of those who received such help ever thanked me or showed any appreciation whatsoever. Quite often they ended up disrespecting me and insulting me for the most absurd reasons.

So do people deserve to be helped? No, they don't!

UNCOMMON: TRANSCENDING THE LIES OF THE MENTAL HEALTH INDUSTRY

I have had religious fanatics, from different christian congregations, and even other religions, asking for my help, and I helped them, in different areas of their life, and the same disrespect and type of insults were given me in return.

Indeed, I have to agree with the motto that people are worthless. People are definitely worthless. But if I could go back in time, I would have done the same things. And even if nowadays, people continue to do the same, I also continue to act as before. The only difference, I would say, is that I don't expect anything anymore as I did before.

Just days ago, I said to a girl who has a speech problem that I am a certified therapist and can, within a few sessions, help her find the subconscious root of the problem and most likely solve it.

This girl spent her entire life with a speech problem, has paid hundreds of dollars in psychologists and psychiatrists, and other doctors, who failed in helping her. And when I offered a specified help for free, she ignored it as if it was dust in the wind.

Then, people wonder how can I be successful in so many areas of my life. Or, as she said, how can I be focused for so many hours.

It should be obvious that I know a lot more about the mind than most therapists, reason why not only can I control mine, but also produce work that leads to the success of others, in truly many areas. But people are truly too stupid to see it. When a person has a speech problem and is offered free certified therapy by a bestselling author, and refuses it, her problem isn't in the speaking or even her subconscious mind. Her problem is that she is too stupid.

Chapter 24: How Can You Feel Younger and Have More Energy?

I am often criticized for using the words stupid too much and on everyone. But this word isn't used lightly. Because I too was stupid for a long period of my life. And nobody ever helped me. I use the word stupid often precisely for this reason. I had to help myself. And now that I offer help for free, based on courses and books I paid, people reject. That is what being stupid truly is!

You are not stupid because you don't know something. You are stupid when you reject the help offered. To reject help offered is the true definition of being stupid. That's why 99,99% are stupid. They are too stupid to see who can help them, they are too stupid to get help, they are too stupid for themselves, quite simply. And if people are that stupid, can you really expect appreciation and respect from them? Surely not! That's delusional! If you help someone and expect that person to help you in return, then you are the stupid.

That is why now, when I give anything to others, that they truly need, more than food or money — solutions to lifelong problems that can shift their fate in a completely new direction —, I don't have a single thought in my mind.

About nine years ago, I had one of my students coming to me, after having already graduated from college, to ask me: "You wrote a letter for me to be able to get a scholarship in the United States. Other teaches did not wrote it. I was accepted because of your letter, despite thousands of other applications that they received, competing against mine. And I am not even from your culture. I am Chinese and you are European. Why did you do it?"

She could not understand that I did it because it's simply my nature. She proceed to give me hints that she was willing to sleep with me, while wondering if I did it because I had feelings for her. And was surprised when I rejected such attention.

She then changed the topic and asked me what do I write the most about, and upon seeing the titles said: "We always thought of you as a very scientific person. We would never imagine you write spiritual books."

Well, yes, there is science to spirituality. I just don't expect others to see it. I actually thought that many of the secret societies understood this science, but they are as stupid as one can be. Not only that, but many suffer from the diseases of arrogance and jealousy. That's worse than being stupid! That is why I don't have much hope invested in such groups or even the academic field.

The more I looked into the many areas of life, and in particular, groups that can make a difference in the world, the more I realized I would have to be the one making that difference.

Groups are composed by people, and people's nature is, to a great extent, decadent, primitive and very limited. But should we then say that this is human nature? It is common! It is stupid! But not very normal. For even monkeys and dogs understand things that humans don't see to understand. Animals appreciate when you give them food. Humans, quite often, not even that.

Once a friend asked me how could he improve his relationships at work, and I told him that people are not driven by logic or common sense. That's why employers and managers realized that chocolate cake and apples lead to more results than meetings, graphics and explanations. People don't care about that!

Then, naturally, the same morons, will say that companies that are modern have games, free coffee and a gym. Because they don't understand that this has nothing to do with the wellbeing of the workers.

Over the past ten years, I have observed through social media, how many of my students grew old. I saw that many are proud of the necklace around their neck with the card of the company, like a proud slave, and proudly post photos of the parties that their company gives twice a year, or the cakes they receive every once in a while. They have sold their soul and youth and dreams to a corporation. And that is very clear in their face! Especially the women! Some of them once beautiful and even working as models, now look like rags.

With me, the opposite has occurred. Many people think I am ten years younger than my real age. They have no clue about my real age or level of life experience. Because I don't grow old like other people. I don't sell my soul to others, I don't

UNCOMMON: TRANSCENDING THE LIES OF THE MENTAL HEALTH INDUSTRY

compromise with any form of bullshit, and I rather work sixteen hours a day and be free, than compromise my future and become a slave. And that's the main difference!

A lot of people ask me how do I manage to keep myself looking so young. But there is nothing I could say to make them understand. Because it is fundamentally related to my relationship with life. My nature is just one element of it. And mental health is surely another. Because betrayals and insults do make me old, but I see such people as ignorant and pathetic. Quite often, their attitude is a clear indicator of how they will end.

Chapter 25: What is The Difference Between Competence and Capacity?

We see that many successful therapies, one way or another, follow the principle of knowing how to shift our nature. But people can't do this on their own. Most people have a sheep mentality. They can't be different if everyone around them looks the same. And so, therapists teach the individual to reprogram his thoughts towards something else but forget that this same individual can't truly change those thoughts, if his environment keeps reinforcing the same thinking patterns.

The problem is often not in the method as much as it is in the what is applied. Because what most of these life coaches, trainers and experts do, is based on their own version of reality, and they commonly know very little about how life works. They assume, and a lot, but they don't really know that much.

Confrontation and running away strategies are included in many successful therapies, but they never obtain significant results if not related with the main purpose. And how can you identify that purpose, if no psychotherapist has a clear definition of mental health?

As I often asked to the psychologists and psychiatrists I met, "If mental health is relative, then the therapy is relative too, which means the procedure is completely arbitrary, leading to high probability of failure". And showing their own failures to therapists is not something they want to deal with. In all these situations, I lost the friendship. But is still amazes me how ignorant people are about the obvious.

I was recently in a seminar on mental health, and many of the attendees where super excited and cooperative with the speaker. And yet, I quickly realized she was a moron with no idea of what she was saying.

Frustrated, I asked as nicely as I could: — "How do you know that what you say is true?"

She answered: — "It's a theory!"

I said to her: — "A theory that has no evidence is actually an opinion."

But she insisted: — "No, it's just a theory"

At that point, everyone jumped on her defense, to justify her, based on their "feelings" and what they "think is right". Because most people are indeed very stupid.

In this group there where accountants, psychologists and business managers. All stupid!

You see, when people can't tell the difference between a theory and an opinion, they belong in a mental hospital, or at least the office of a therapist, as a patient, not giving seminars to others. But sadly, this wasn't the only case I met like this.

This woman was from Holland. But shortly before meeting her, I met another, from Lithuania, who was also ignorant about many things, but was convinced that she had a mission of spreading her bullshit to others.

I didn't care much about the situation of this Lithuanian women, until I saw her talking on radio and television. She had put so many efforts to be noticed, that she eventually got the attention she wanted. And that's when those who make me sad, also make me worried.

Many of the people speaking publicly, should not be heard by anyone.

What do we get when the stupid come out as experts and spread their own bullshit to the rest of the world? Even more stupidity!

Then people wonder why the world is so broken. Well, entitlement is one of the causes. Just because someone feels entitled to speak to others, or write books, doesn't mean she should.

Quite a lot of the people that come to me asking how to write or sell books, insult me, when I ask "about what?", and they answer: "I don't know?"

Are they comparing my writing to going to the toilet? Because it's not a need or nonsense. There is a lot of background work to it. They just don't see it and don't care.

UNCOMMON: TRANSCENDING THE LIES OF THE MENTAL HEALTH INDUSTRY

As the obsession of many people in this world is towards themselves, they invoke their narcissistic entitlement as the only justification needed to, in the name of peace and help, create destruction.

Not long after this seminar, I had two psychologists insisting in having me doing a seminar about mental health. I refused!

They couldn't understand why I refused. They thought nobody would ever refuse an opportunity to show their talents and promote their own books. They even told me they could pay me, and that I could promote my books in the seminar. But I kept refusing! And they couldn't understand why.

I refused because I knew that they were too stupid to see the value of what I had to share. They could sense the importance of it, but they couldn't see the real value. And that's the part most people, absorbed by their narcissistic greed, can't see. I don't do anything for those who read my books or listen to me. I do it to change the world. If I sense that those who get my words may create destruction using what I give them, then I won't give them anything.

Surely, my books are available to anyone, but there is a technique, a code, in my writing, that can only go through certain people.

Narcissists can't understand what I write, much less apply it. I know because I have tested giving my books to different types of people, just to see how they interpret them. Surely, my technique has been improved over the years, but it is a very specific and unique technique.

I noticed that musicians in particular, can see it, because they tell me that reading my books makes them feel different — empowered, smarter, confident, sharper. And this occurs because a large portion of my secret technique is applied through the heart.

I spent an entire life developing the ability to connect mind and heart. And naturally, those who have empathy and compassion, get a huge boost through my words, even when I speak, while those who are self-centered are constantly trying to get key phrases in me that they can use on others to hypnotize them.

That is, to a great extent, what frightened the communists when I was teaching in China, because they would look at the surveillance cameras inside the classroom, and, as they themselves told me, meticulously analyze me, but not see any reason as to why I had such power over the students, and was able to change their mind so easily.

Some of them, psychologists trained in the United States, would even enter my class to observe me, and where as clueless as anyone else. That scared them!

I did have a tremendous power over the students, but it would always remain invisible to the radar of the communists, psychologists and anyone else who tried to study it. Because most of what I know is, quite simply, not from this world.

When I speak about mental health, I am not just speaking about the brain, but the whole view of what being a human means. That is why what I say works. You or anyone else, does not need to understand it.

We may be scared by that which we can't understand, but why aren't people scared of what their psychiatrists are doing? Does the label of psychiatrist makes them immune to criticism?

Let us not forget that many of the most dangerous criminals in concentration camps during the nazi occupation were scientists, and many of those scientists were recruited by the secret services to work in the United States and Russia, among other countries, like Egypt. Many others escaped to South America, where they continued on working, as doctors and pharmacists.

History has shown us that there is no reason for us to trust certificates and social hierarchies.

Chapter 26: Why Some People Love Conflict and Drama?

Taking into consideration that our mind is connected to our heart, the simplest thing one can do to shift his attention consists of changing his emotions. And this can be accomplished with music.

There is nothing wrong with listening to angry music when we feel angry, or depressed music when we feel depressed. Music helps us get in contact with our emotions, which then allows dissolving them while processing our thoughts more clearly. It is the opposite of suppressing our emotions, which leads us to become less rational.

Surely, if we constantly listen to music that uplifts our emotions, that makes it easier to confront our problems rather than escaping them. This said, what is the realistic meaning in feeling low and depressed?

The sensation of "feeling low" or "feeling down", is related to the sensation that we are in a negative frequency. Like with any other disease, it is the way of our body telling us that we are not living in a healthy way.

We may feel this way when remembering negative experience, or looking backwards at the bad things that happen to us, or that are happening in the world. The news and the movies constantly prey on our anxieties, worries and fears, because these emotions paralyze us and keep us addicted to a certain level of consumption. But as with sugar, pleasure doesn't mean that adding more of it will do us good. Pleasure in pain and suffering is, quite frankly, a sign that the mind has went astray and out of its way.

A person who feels sadistic or masochist pleasure is surely sick. There is no way to debate this rationally. But many do want to rationalize it, because they don't want to consider themselves to be mentally ill, neither do they want to consider that about their acquaintances or the vast majority of the world, which is very sadistic. Everyone loves to see death, blood and fights.

How many times have you seen a physical or verbal confrontation between two individuals that attracted the attention of many, and in which nobody interfered to stop it?

It is very normal because most people are very abnormal.

Sadism could be considered a natural trait but it's actually common and not natural, because sadism is part of that mental illness that many share. Whenever people see destruction, it hooks them through that sadistic and adrenaline need.

It is important to mention as well, that just as the more years an alcoholic has been consuming alcohol, the more challenging it is for him to stop, as his whole body will react to it, the same happens to people who can't stop eating meat or smoking or drinking coffee. And the same also applies to this adrenaline coming from aggression.

If people systematically watch aggressive movies, and brutalization in video games and other means they come in contact with, even if just visually, the more addicted they will be to the emotion.

It occurs, nonetheless, that just with any other addiction, their body gets accustomed to the dose that is provided, always needing for me. So just as many drug addicts die from overdose, most human beings also grow increasingly needy for this adrenaline rush.

The addiction to drama, for example, is related to it. So, to say that women enjoy drama is absurd. Many women are indeed addicted to drama, just as men are addicted to confrontations and competition with other men, because that's how people are wired to behave. Mentally, they don't know how to express their emotions in any other way.

It may seem like a paradox, but it's surely an interesting one, when you see that many professional fighter and heavy metal band members, are actually very social and friendly. This occurs because they channel their emotions towards a specific activity.

UNCOMMON: TRANSCENDING THE LIES OF THE MENTAL HEALTH INDUSTRY

Most people don't have this level of channeling. Their personal life consist of routines. And so, whoever goes on their way, gets their emotions.

More and more people are acting extremely aggressive these days, because they are mentally ill. Any attempt at controlling them by force, will either lead to life imprisonment, a bullet in their head, or a mental house.

Does that mean that such people are wrong to act aggressively? Not exactly! I have noticed that this need for drama and aggression is present in many police officers and security guards as well, who often escalate a normal situation with disrespect and abuse of authority, on purpose, because they are addicted to this same adrenaline.

This planet is very sick because of this need to be high all the time, with aggression and violence. People are literally addicted to pain and violence. As such, they then compensate their competitive drive through narcissistic entitlement. Which is part of the same competitive and violent mindset.

Chapter 27: Why is There Evil?

Most of the offices of mental therapists are occupied by some of the most dangerous criminals in the world. In some cases that I have encountered, I actually wondered if these individuals themselves where mental patients and not certified therapists. Because they acted as if they where psychopathic, even in my presence.

Some believe that in the highest ranks of society, politicians and other influential members of society are engaged in satanic rituals that sacrifice humans to extract their blood and consume the adrenochrome — a substance that is released by the heart when someone is under extreme fear and stress — and that doesn't surprise me. Many FBI officers have confirmed it. And I am here explaining to you why it happens.

The higher one goes in this decadent social hierarchy, the higher will be the need for extreme emotions.

Parachuting and bungee jumping would be a better option and more healthy too. But I believe that when people are corrupt and have enough money not to worry about justice, they extend the limits of what they shouldn't do as much as they can.

That wouldn't be very different from the Chinese and Vietnamese or Korean, who burn dogs alive or eat rats and fish alive to obtain the same chemicals.

Human cruelty for the pleasure of killing has always been a constant throughout history. We may blame the Mayans for their human sacrifices, but the Roman Empire used their Coliseum to give the people the same pleasure of seeing others being tortured and eaten alive throughout the whole empire. And they actually saw this as a way to maintain peace and avoid rebellions.

Then, the many monarchs and dictators of the world did the same, by murdering people in public squares, and burning them alive. That paralyzing panic was addictive to the masses.

We didn't come a long way from there. People are still as primitive as their grandparents. Violence is still greatly motivated by boring lives and addiction to sadism.

Is that evil? Yes!

Is that Satanic? Yes!

Are most Christians, Muslims, Hindus and members from many other religions, evil and Satanic? Yes, they surely are! I just showed you why! Any religion that uses violence as a means to gain support is sick.

The Saudis who want people to be decapitated in the name of religion, are mentally ill, and as much as the christians who get gratification in knowing that non-christians will suffer for all of eternity burning in hell.

Any ideology based on the gratification of death and suffering can only be followed by sick people. And that's what usually happens, because you can't attract a large following unless you connect the values of the religion with the sick minds of the followers.

When a religion doesn't have this sadistic satisfaction, it has to invent it. All religions end up vilifying some group of society, as a form of dramatizing itself.

In many other habited planets, movies in which everything is good and nothing bad happens are fine. But not on earth! Here, a movie without conflict won't be even considered a movie.

There must always be conflict on earth, either it's an inner conflict, imaginary, or against someone or some group, or even some entity. That addiction to conflict has to be present for Earthly humans to feel human. And that's exactly what makes humans a primitive humanoid race.

To give atomic weapons to humans is like giving a knife or a pistol to a monkey. Humans are not evolved enough to be handed the power to murder and destroy. The human nature at the moment is destructive enough.

UNCOMMON: TRANSCENDING THE LIES OF THE MENTAL HEALTH INDUSTRY

Our evolution as a collective at the moment, has to go through this understanding, without which, no method of healing the mind will be effective.

Chapter 28: How Do Brain Waves Influence Our Emotional State?

Our brainwaves always show our emotions in a vibrational pattern. It can be measured and quantified as well. Because we are fundamentally composed of energy, and our thoughts have energy too.

Meditation and other activities that manage to balance our brainwaves, do produce effects in our emotions. Therefore, playing music, doing sports, going for a walk or climbing, are all activities that show benefits for our mental health, no matter how simple or complex our condition is.

When we are high on life, happy with our experiences, we do feel much better, at least during that moment. Reason why people get so excited with certain activities like making new friends, traveling, and falling in love. And there is something particularly special to falling in love that other activities don't offer. The sense of emotional attachment felt after that initial experience, maintains the same emotion for a longer period of time. But we naturally need to feel safe in our relationship, because otherwise that sense of attachment can't be produced. And so, people fall in love quickly, but also fall out of love equally fast, if they don't feel secure about the future with a certain person.

It is, however, easy to make someone fall out of love by using fears against the person. So, people fall out of love, not only due to their insecurities but also imagined fears. One needs to be mature at many levels to be able to acquire a balanced life. And this is why we can say that our mental health depends to a great extent on how much we understand life.

You can see if a person is normal or mentally ill just by measuring his brainwaves and that is done in many hospitals with the use of the electroencephalogram. But we can also measure changes in the brain, by making the individual interact at an emotional level with his own memory. And that is how we measure the development of a situation.

When psychiatrists decide to give electrical shocks to patients, they're giving up on their theories to apply a more direct approach and change the brainwaves by force. But that force disrupts the natural process, and as result, the individual may seem better on the surface, but his ability to remember is damaged in the process.

Does amnesia justify the cure? And what is a cured patient without a past?

You can't detach the individual from his past and his traumas. And that's not necessarily a pessimist approach, unless we consider that the past determines the future.

Whenever we start justifying our life with our past, that's when we challenge ourselves against our potential. And this potential can only be unveiled once we confront the barriers that manifest in front of us.

All fears can be overcome. And once they are, are they still fears? Not anymore!

A whole change to our personality is formed around both what we know we can do and what we know that what we can't do. And so, if one wishes to be rehabilitated, he needs first to increase his potential in some area of life to be able to transfer these skills to other areas.

Children learn about the world and themselves by interacting with the world. And the same applies to adults. It's through our interactions with the world that we get to know ourselves better.

That doesn't mean that we must judge ourselves accordingly.

If we judge all the animals by their ability to swim, a monkey won't get great results when compared to crocodiles. But if we measure animals by their ability to climb a tree, monkeys will do better.

When we look at our mind and personality, and even our appearance, it is obvious that some locations, some people, and some activities will make us more successful and happier than others. And if we are doing well, do we really suffer any type of mental illness or trauma?

UNCOMMON: TRANSCENDING THE LIES OF THE MENTAL HEALTH INDUSTRY

Unless a person is very sadistic, at a psychopathic level, a cure is relatively at reach and certainly possible under these circumstances.

Chapter 29: Why is Point of View So Important For Our Well-being?

One of the main ways of solving a problem consists of observing it from different angles. We can read about it from different perspectives, both scientific and religious, but also test different and alternative solutions, such as eating a more healthy diet, based on vegetables and fruits, for the body can heal itself, if given the opportunity to do so.

The way our world is built tends to hide this fact, even though present in all scientific research, because if people searched for alternatives, the mainstream solutions that they know will lose strength, and that means that conventional therapies may be abandoned in favor of more efficient ones.

The world doesn't evolve based on results, but financial investments. And there is a huge investment in drugs by the pharmaceutical industry. This industry, one way or another, control the educational system, from which the mental health experts emerge. Therefore, the system is conditioned and manipulated in a certain way, not because it is more truthful but rather more profitable.

One of the reasons why I am so careful with my diet is related to my mental health. I noticed a clear parallel between eating processed food and getting depressed, and eating fresh fruits and vegetables, and in particular, non-cooked meals, and feeling better with myself.

We can justify these emotions and thoughts with many other circumstances, but I have tested times enough over the years, to verify that the correlation is direct. Even though our negative experiences can lead us to depression, the effects of depression are higher when a person isn't following a healthy diet.

I don't know what to say to those who consider drinking alcohol and smoking drugs is a great way to be creative. I have never seen quality work produced by such people. But I did notice that my writing and thoughts are clearer and more organized when I am being careful with my diet.

On the other hand, when we observe a pharmaceutical drug, what is that if not a combination of elements that can be found in our food?

Being uncommon then may make us sound weird and crazy, but does lead to answers most just don't see. And how uncommon can you be when healing yourself?

If you seek advantages within your negative experiences, you can obtain positive outcomes, at least, in your personality. Traumas do make us more aware of our self-worth and our needs.

I'm not saying that the trauma is necessary, but rather that we can see it as a barrier or an advantage, depending on how we wish to look at it. If we look at positively, we can forgive ourselves more easily and then shift our situation with a new attitude.

This perspective is promoted by taoism — all that is bad can become good, and vice-versa. Although it does help to make the transition, if we dream and envision a better outcome for ourselves.

Ideas move us towards a certain goal and inspire us to do better.

We see what our eyes can see, but we act and accept our difficulties according to what we belief. And so, if we learn to see life from many different perspectives, by talking to different people and learning from different backgrounds and cultures, we gradually start seeing our difficulties in new ways.

Action follows the strongest ideas but ideas motivate us, and motivation creates speed, which leads to persistence.

This said, the more you wait for something to occur, the less likely what you want will manifest itself. But, if you do what you feel, plan it, organize it and fight as much as you can to obtain it, then that speed, will generate its own energy and strength. Everything else that doesn't match your focus will collapse, namely, sadness and fears.

Love is aligned with such attitude. When we are more extroverted, we find more rapidly those whom we love, and we also love more easily. Our determination to feel happy feeds our dreams and creates better realities.

People often think they need to solve their problems first before they can dream, but that doesn't correspond to how life works. Many times, when you are achieving your goals, you will not have time to even think about your problems. You have to make choices. And choosing to keep problems doesn't seem reasonable at that point.

If you keep yourself focused on your problems, you will even gradually detach from the thoughts that keep you anxious, stressed, depressed, and ill.

The opposite, as in making decisions with anger and anxiety or fears, is what leads us to have accidents and make crucial mistakes.

Luck is always the result of many probabilities coming in our favor, but you can only head that way, if you shift your focus towards your dreams.

Chapter 30: What Types of People You Cannot Help?

Before helping ourselves, others, or seeking for help, or even considering such thoughts, we must realize that only those who can help themselves, can be helped.

Nobody can provide assistance when such is invalidated. We can help as much as someone is willing to accept help. And this apparent contradiction brings us to another problematic related to the topic of mental health: One can only be healed if he is healthy enough to be healed.

Does this mean that those who refuse help can't be helped? Basically, yes. Narcissists and psychopaths typically don't see anything wrong with their behavior, and even fear to change and lose their "shields and weapons", and therefore, they will refuse therapy.

There are two kinds of people that can't be helped and two that can. Those that can't be helped have been, somehow, deeply hurt in the past or too many times, and also feel betrayed by the ones who were supposed to help them and protect them, or someone they loved. And those who can be helped, usually help others, and in doing so, can see positive outcomes coming from the acceptance of help. They develop a positive perspective to life, built out of a healthy and loving exchange of experiences with others, most of which emerging from healthy social interactions.

Now, how much of a good life one needs to have to change habits?

We would have to look at those who recover from substance abuse or childhood traumas to understand this. Because we can easily see that the percentage is small in both cases.

A narcissist, for example, has a learned behavior and developed a sadistic drive that he or she can't replace with anything else. The traumas that program the narcissist to act that way, come with a set of reasons, that the narcissist would have to abdicate to change.

Basically, the narcissist would have to decide to be empathic, and they can't be. Because they spent an entire life protecting themselves from harm. For the narcissist to change, he or she would have to feel safe. And that never happens! The narcissist would have to necessarily face the consequences of being a nice person and maybe get hurt, and that won't happen either.

This paradox of the narcissist wanting to live a good life and fearing it, is what keeps them in such mindset for a whole lifetime, ending up destroyed by their own view of themselves.

When we look at substance abuse, the situation is not so drastic, although it depends on how powerful the drug is on the individual taking it. And we can't neglect the powerful effects of sugar and coffee as two of the most powerful drugs, because quite a lot of people are addicted to food and coffee as well.

The vast majority of the population is so dependent on stimulants and excitement to balance their difficult life, that they end up maintaining themselves in a cycle that even their therapist can't solve. A great number of the world population has been, at least once, in a therapeutic session or has taken antidepressants before.

Many would attribute this phenomenon to social development and the complexities of our modern lifestyle, but even though it is a reasonable explanation for this trend, it does not correspond to the truth. The greatest truth about this phenomenon is also the hardest to accept, namely, that people are being pushed towards insanity through a specific set of lies that they are being told to follow, and that they do follow for lack of better alternatives.

Our world is driven by private corporations and interests, that end up influencing political decisions, and even corrupting many organizations. Greed and profit are in control of the society in which we live today, and psychotropics do sell a lot. Some psychiatric drugs have generated over $4 billion to the pharmaceutical industry.

Chapter 31: Is Insanity Contagious?

Many people wonder if the fast spread of depression and other mental illnesses may be contagious. And yes, it is. As with the problem of a virus, what we see here is that it can't be detected soon enough to allow ourselves to be protected.

Quite a lot of the people who cause distress in others suffer from some form of mental illness themselves. Happy and healthy people do not enjoy bringing problems to others.

I am not saying that those who suffer from bipolar disorders or schizophrenia are guilty of their condition, or can infect others, but rather that those who are obsessed with their traumas, tend to dramatize their relationships, by seeing danger where there is none and attacking those who are not dangerous to them.

It is said that the most fundamental definition of insanity consists of doing the opposite of what a healthy being would. And so, when a person is practicing something that is potentially harmful for the mind or body, this person could be considered insane.

Is watching TV, according to this principle, an insane act? Definitely!

On the other hand, we shouldn't neglect the ones that assimilate trauma as part of their daily routine, such as physicians, nurses, psychiatrist, psychologists and dentists. As they are being confronted daily with high levels of emotional pressure, stress and anxiety, end up being the most vulnerable to a breakdown and then to develop mental disorders.

There is a high percentage of people in the medical field who commit suicide and that's not a coincidence.

The tendency to hallucinate or develop neurotic compensations, also comes as a need to escape emotional suffering. Reason why, it is more common than many would imagine, that psychiatrists and psychologists are under the same effects of the drugs they prescribe to their own patients.

Quite often, the help that is provided is in the same level of beliefs of the one providing it. Therefore, if a certain therapist trusts the effects of drugs more than he trusts his own procedures, we can't expect much technical efficiency in what he does. Such efficiency depends a lot on the capacity to feel empathy for another person. But what if the patient doesn't feel any empathy for herself and her situation?

Quite a lot of people need attention more than they need help. Many people complain about problems, unwilling to receive solutions, while demanding attention through a victimization that actually reflects lack of responsibility. And often, this comes from a fear of self-analysis, related to an already very low self-esteem. In other words, such people fear the guilt that consciousness of the self brings them.

The therapist that doesn't risk losing the patient by making him face the consequences of his own actions is not doing a very good job.

Many patients seek for the sympathy of their therapists and see them as a substitute to their parents, especially if the patient is a narcissist. But quite often, those who seek the help of a therapist, have somehow failed in helping themselves.

If we exclude the mental illnesses that are of an organic nature, and which are very few when compared to the many that emerge from certain life experiences and habits, we come to the conclusion that most of the problems could be eliminated with a proper self-analysis.

This is why many of such people seek for the help of hypnotists and other professionals, that can help them get in touch with their true self. And there's nothing wrong with that. But it is indeed interesting that people go to a therapist for lack of better answers, and end up having to change their habits to change their results in life.

What to do then when people can't change their habits and overcome their depressions?

UNCOMMON: TRANSCENDING THE LIES OF THE MENTAL HEALTH INDUSTRY

In Suicide Prevention Clinics, the overall strategy consists in helping the patient change focus to other things in life, so that his thinking becomes less absorbed by the daily routines. And yet, when the patient stops showing to appointments, everyone assumes that he or she couldn't follow-up with the suggestions provided. Almost never do experts consider that their approach may simply not be suitable.

Suicide may be a choice but not as much as it is expected when everything else fails.

Chapter 32: How Can a Subgroup Impact Our Mental Health?

The mental health level of a person can be measured through his or her willingness to live. The more plans the person has and the more significant such plans are, the more healthy that person will be, which is to say, the drive to survive will be strong.

We can therefore conclude that determinism and persistent is a quality of the healthiest. Depressive and apathetic individuals can't persist towards their goals for a long period of time.

This premise leads us to many deductions, such as the fact that you can increase the motivation of an individual towards a stronger willingness for life by giving him a goal that is emotionally significant, such as learning how to play guitar, finding someone to love, or taking a course related to a dream career.

We often criticize those who are different but being different, or uncommon, is actually one of the most reliable mechanisms of self-defense when we are addressing our mind.

Those who explore their own talents, learn to enjoy solitude and can make friends with personalities that are unusual, but not in any way bad, and become more equipped to deal with the challenges that life throws at them.

We can very well say too, that the many subgroups and movements that have emerged from society, predominately in recent years, are healthy answers to an escapism that society itself does not provide. And we certainly want those groups to be characterized by their fashion and music, rather than their violence. Because, again, gang violence is just another form of wanting to belong to society and even though an unreasonable one.

We do need to be different, not just in cultures and skin color, in appearance or clothing, but also in our desires, goals and personality. And we need to explore that through the many routes provided by society.

The idea that we must accept the world as it is, is actually very unhealthy, although promoted by many people who themselves can't change anything.

If you ask an entrepreneur or a politician what he thinks of life, he will certainly not tell you that we must accept things as they are, or he wouldn't be able to achieve anything, not even recognition for something.

Self-awareness may very well be a consequence of frustration, and this frustration a symptom associated with depression, but one doesn't just move upwards by conforming to that which he doesn't like, and he won't change if he learns to enjoy it.

You don't need much to throw a person into his own death, if you deprive him of the only necessary elements to build an identity. That means forcing the person to accept the world as a duality, as in choose A or B, and as if not choosing A meant automatically that you must choose B.

I see people constantly falling into this trap when talking to me. They will say:

— "Oh, you don't think A? So why do you believe B?"

They cannot understand that life is not only A or B. And that's another form of stupidity that leads to insanity, when you are so obsessed with a duality that you can't see anything else.

We have learned to anchor our emotions to social elements that don't define us as we are, and then we wonder why we are so miserable, as we can't see it.

Many times, people become severely ill because they were thrown from an A-situation to a B-situation, that they weren't prepare to deal with or didn't expect.

One day a person loses his job, his wife divorces him and takes the kids away, and his friends, afraid that bad luck may be contagious, disappear too. Suddenly, the social image disappears because everything such individual was depended on, in order to maintain his social image, has vanished. And without that social image, his life has no meaning.

UNCOMMON: TRANSCENDING THE LIES OF THE MENTAL HEALTH INDUSTRY

It's difficult to talk about options when the whole structure of the personality has been corrupted by society itself.

The only way to solve this fundamental problem consists in either rebuilding what was lost or rebuilding the personality with a new set of beliefs. And we know how hard that can be.

Chapter 33: How To Deal With Negative Thoughts?

In a world with self-destructive tendencies and abnormal perspectives about reality, in which criticism and anger are often more appreciated and worshipped than love and compassion, the only way out consists in using a social mask. People then have to pretend to be someone they're not in order to be respected.

This is why those under depression put more efforts and will smile more to hide their sorrow and sadness. They are anxious about distracting others, fearing that otherwise their lack of self-esteem may be noticed, leading to segregation and discrimination.

If they could, they would hide in public sight, and they do hide, but in other ways.

The psychologic feeling of being trapped comes afterwards, from the need to have a social life. That's when the antisocial personality starts developing furthermore.

The worst nightmare of someone with an antisocial personality is to be left alone to his thoughts and depression, but it is also this same mindset that invalidates the capability to be social.

With the inability to deal with suicidal tendencies and social anxiety comes the potential to develop insomnia and other health related issues. The outside eventually becomes a reflection of what can't be accepted inside.

The situation becomes worse in time. When people attach to delusional versions of themselves, they tend to suffer more with stress.

Deep down, they know the beliefs they were raise with are lies, but they can't realize it, even when their behaviors aren't coherent with their emotions.

- People often say that money is not important, but feed the fear of losing a job;

- They say happiness comes from within, but anxiously desire to travel;

- They say friendship matters more than material things, but always want the latest laptop.

Even though sadness and depression are normal emotional states, just like happiness is, there's a reason for them to be currently more prominent, and it is due to the delusional paradigms that conduct so many people to their confusions.

Most people gave up having control over their own future. And from this point onward, became at the mercy of a system and what it provides. But it is a corrupt and sick system, reason why it doesn't work well.

If the world operated under normal values and principles, we wouldn't have so many sick people, reason why depression and many other illnesses tend to be less common in certain cultures and societies, namely rural places of Southeast Asia and among the aboriginal tribes of South America.

The only way out comes from within, by looking at our core nature. And the necessary steps to get out are the same for everyone, either when receiving help, helping others or helping ourselves.

The cure for depression is love towards ourselves and our world.

Human beings have different background experiences and personalities, and therefore react differently to their challenges in life, but everyone processes information equally in a commonly filtered reality and which obeys basic principles, such as gravity.

If reality isn't relative, adjusting to it shouldn't be as well. And this adjusting requires starting from a common ground of beliefs allowing agreement, respect and compassion.

Chapter 34: Can Love Be a Healing Force?

Love is an emotion that can be acknowledged and felt both in giving and receiving. And the more lonely people are, the more they feel the need to experience it.

Most people may not realize that they are lonely, but the lack of physical contact, the lack of face-to-face interactions, and the constant use of social media for any type of communication, shows us that people are indeed lonely.

This feeling can't be overcome with the illusion of a communication online, because it is not the same as being next to the person we are talking with.

When are next to someone, there is a lot more than words being exchange, there are emotions, perceptions and a whole non-verbal communication. That can't be obtained through typing.

In general, interactions have been reduced to personal gratification. But is it difficult to show appreciation for someone?

If you offer a toy or a chocolate to a child, you can easily make the child smile. However, if you offer flowers to an adult, that doesn't always happen, unless the person has already built a certain relationship with you. But how can that happen if people are isolating themselves more and hiding behind screens?

As the behavior itself shows, depends on personal perceptions. In other words, people are being driven more by their inner beliefs than the hypothesis of getting to know someone different and experiencing something new. People are literally replicating their own beliefs, like hamsters in a wheel.

The appearance of dating apps has reinforced this behavior. By being more superficial, people now systematically reinforce what they already know.

If we inverse this paradigm, to see how the individual changes through the interactions with others, we see that the change comes as a crystallization of what already is.

People are growing more arrogant and stupid at the same time. They don't know anything about life, but the repetition of outcomes, makes them believe that they do.

That is like comparing your house to the planet and assuming that, because you know the corners of your own house, you already know the whole planet as well.

Most people think that, because their outcomes in life are always the same, they are correct. They don't think that their outcomes are predictable because their decisions are always the same.

What this causes is two things:

- People can easily be brainwashed and controlled, because they won't change the paradigm imprinted in their mind;

- It is now more difficult to cure any mental illness, because the individual is both convinced that he is correct, and keeps through daily habits repeating the same cycle of decisions, behaviors and beliefs.

Certainly, you can't expect anything different if you keep repeating the same behaviors.

Chapter 35: Why Is Chaos In Your Life Essential To True Growth?

Many times people ask me how do I make friends easily and in any country, and are surprised when I explain it in simple terms. Because they are so obsessed with their own views of the world, that they never stop to think that their sheep mentality, of always following a herd, doesn't produce the same results as when they are in control of a self-created chaos.

I explain. This chaos that most people are so afraid of, namely, related to the possibility of being rejected and ostracized by others, is necessary when you want to meet new people that you never expected to find. And this can only occur when you destroy the patterns of your habits.

You can do this by organizing different types of events. Some events will work well, while others won't. But you can see, as you go along, what type of people are attracted to which events, and with whom you can be friends with.

As you keep doing these things, you will see that most people may not feel any empathy with you, but those who do will become your new friends.

This is how you create a positive outcome out of chaos. But nobody teaches you this because the last thing society wants is chaos.

If you are able to disrupt the system as a leader of your own life, you become unpredictable, and you won't need psychologists anymore. And that's why nobody will ever suggest you that. As soon as you become successful outside the mainstream, you become an undesirable person.

I am hated whatever I go, because I can create subgroups, and act as a leader of this subgroup against the majority of the group, and through that manipulation of interests, invert the power structure to my side, forcing the previous order to adjust to the new order. And this works better when the old order is outdated, subversive, suppressive and ineffective.

You can't really do this when people are happy with a system, even if the system doesn't work and the people are too stupid to see it.

That is why I was feared in China. It was too easy for me to do this and invert the power structure, which as a foreigner was threatening to the communists. But the only reason why I could do it easily, is because their whole system is corrupt.

Any truth can sparkle a fire in the mind of those who are ready to be awaken.

In other countries, I was seen not as a threat, but a prophet, because people could sense the same. And yet, even if they were Europeans, they were as brainwashed as the Chinese communists.

People can't accept that which frightens them the most, and many are afraid of almost everything they are not familiar with, including compassion, empathy and love.

You can't really explain this in a country like Lithuania, where most people are constantly considering committing suicide and are total imbeciles with outsiders. Xenophobia is a very obvious indications of a sick people. And Lithuanians are extremely xenophobic. Which makes them the most insane nation of Earth.

The solution that many countries have found to suicide was an assisted euthanasia. Therefore, following the same logic, it would be reasonable to euthanize the whole country of Lithuania. Although, when we expand this logic, we see how cruel it may seem.

This is why, just as you can't compare a country with an individual, by following the same premises, you can only test the validity of a premise when doing it. E.g., just like a person who wishes to commit suicide needs a change of paradigms, the country of Lithuania needs to disappear.

Is this a radical approach? Well, I would say to you that people are obsessed with their beliefs as much as they are with their culture. Both things are transitory, imaginary and ridiculous to maintain when suppressive.

Chapter 36: Is Jealousy a Symptom of Psychiatric Disorder?

Unfortunately, many people have wrong beliefs about life with which they make their decisions. They rarely consider their beliefs to be false. That would imply that their personality is wrong. It is an attack on their ego that they aren't willing to take. And so, it becomes natural for them to justify the outcome by seeing guilt in others or some act of criminality in them.

For example, some people hate me because I know more than them. Instead of assuming that they are too ignorant, they assume that I am obtaining my information from some secret agency. If they like me, they may think I am a genius or that God talks to me. Their justifications are always guided by their emotions towards the outside and never the inside.

The same occurs if I have a lifestyle they envy. If they like me, they will say I'm lucky. If they don't, they will accuse me of crimes they can't even prove. Again, they never assume that they are too lazy to work as hard as I did to obtain the same.

Following along these patterns, many believe that value is somehow a secret you must protect and keep from sharing, reason why they ask many things but answer nothing about themselves. Poor nations in particular, show this habit in their people. These people are so used to scarcity, they think happiness is a limited value too, just as gold or cash. When you smile more, they get mad.

Again, the country of the crazies and psychos — Lithuania, shows this trait abundantly. They are all so miserably embedded in self-hatred and xenophobia, that they think those who smile too much are stupid. They never think that they themselves are the stupid.

Following the same belief, many hide their happiness. They hide what makes them proud, their relationships and their knowledge. It's ridiculous but quite common in many people who are mentally ill.

You can see that, as people go downwards in their mental health, they become more and more self-absorbed. And yes, many meditation practices, for promoting such behaviors, end up causing worse problems in those who already suffer with depression.

The same applies with therapists. I never considered that a therapist could lead someone to commit suicide, until I found that to be common among Lithuanian psychologists.

A proper investigation would lead many of them to jail, and quite certainly, but I doubt any government would have the courage to face such scandal and be known by the rest of the world as a country of mental health criminals.

We can look at the whole planet and transfer this example to other nations, and it becomes clear that, the fear of confronting problems is a cause of mental illnesses at many levels, especially, when those in whom we trust are the problem — the government, the therapists, the educational system, and so on.

You do a great favor to yourself by being uncommon in a country where what is common is to be insane.

Sadly, however, that also leads you to being psychologically bullied.

Disrespect and insults are common in Lithuania, whenever a person doesn't fit the paradigm of the many stupid of that country. And that, I must say, is the number one priority that leads those who emigrate to other nations to seek a better life, most likely, more than money itself.

Governments will never stop the emigration of the healthiest, if they focus only on the financial situation of their country, and not the state of the culture as well. But a country will always be poor, for as long as it is focused on basic needs, such as money.

You can't do much for the culture, if your priority is on the system itself.

UNCOMMON: TRANSCENDING THE LIES OF THE MENTAL HEALTH INDUSTRY

This said, it is certainly difficult to change your focus, when everything around you looks like shit. But easy, when you change your environment. And contrary to what many think, it is easier to get richer when you are happy than it is when you are depressed.

Have you ever tried to work after a break up or divorce? Was it the same? Obviously not! And well, the same applies to nations who focus on their money rather than their culture and the happiness of their people.

What makes the United States rich, for example, is not the fact that it has a vast amount of wealth, but its culture of opportunities, that embraces a vast amount of different other cultures.

The majority of its immigrants would never consider to go back to their country, because they wouldn't encounter the same amount of opportunities.

Opportunity means freedom to choose and that freedom only appears when you are in a rich environment, rich in interactions, different personalities, different values, and so on.

It is the variety of different interests merging in the United States, that make it such a great nation and despite the many problems.

If we do the inverse comparison, we see that the same applies to our personal life. You grow and change more easily when you have the chance to be yourself, and interact with people that can help you find that true and happy self.

If you go to a psychologist that puts efforts in assimilating you back into the herd, that therapist is certainly an imbecile that doesn't know anything about how life works. Most likely, him or her, is a loser too. And that is why you must always focus on people who succeeded in overcoming challenges before you can ask for an advice.

You should not trust someone just because this person has a paper certifying whatsoever. Systems don't prove anything but themselves.

Chapter 37: Why Life is a Mirror Reflecting Your Inner World?

Everything that occurs in life has a dual side. If you don't give love, you can't receive it. For example, you can only appreciate a landscape if you put your attention on what you love in that landscape and allow its beauty to be part of you. In essence, it is when you choose to be happy that you are willing to accept happiness. You can't get that when you are closed in your mind and heart.

This is why narcissists can't feel love. They can't love as well.

You may often hear from people that rich individuals are sad or that money creates loneliness, but this isn't true. The truth isn't relative to having or not whatsoever in a materialistic sphere of perception, but to how you handle that which is given to you. How you handle your environment defines your sadness and happiness.

Just as a clean house improves your mood and a dirty house can leave you depressed, clean and good quality clothes improve your self-esteem, while dirty smelly rags can make you feel worthless. Money does contribute to our well-being but only to the extent in which we use it effectively. In this sense, the way we make money also affects how we see ourselves.

You are certainly more proud of making money by being smart than by being an opportunist without moral or a criminal. But many people forget this in their ambition to obtain more money, and then sell their peace of mind for superficial goals.

That may work in a short period of time, but in a long run, one has to constantly be getting more to erase the sense of guilt.

This is why morally acquired money is better to built self-worth, just as sex with love, purchases directed at our own well-being, and a good diet, all contribute for our mental health.

If money was bad, homeless people would be the happiest in the world.

It is the disconnection between our true self and the sources of happiness that truly leads us downwards into sadness and depression.

In the same way, we can say the opposite, e.g., that fruitful interactions produce happiness and a better state of mind. And so, sharing, leads to happiness. However, the amount of what you share is proportional to what you can give or receive. You can't share happiness, well-being and inspiration, while feeling sad, unhealthy and depressed.

The observations we make of the reality we see in others also define our choices. And people do see different things, according to the nature of reality they keep replicating.

If we must explain the concept of being positive, I would say that it is based not in the positive aspect of it, but the ability to differentiate states of mind, and how they lead to very different results and behaviors.

For example, most poor people assume that it is the possession of something that leads them to their happiness, because they have little, but the rich know that it is what they can do with it that makes them happy. And so, while the poor are focused on possessing a yacht, for example, the rich are focused on where they can go with that boat.

The same I could say about those who ask me how to make money with books and music. It doesn't matter how smart and talented they are, because they will never reach my level of success. And they won't ever reach it for a very simple reason: They are trying to get it from a selfish and poor mindset.

They are looking at the money as their goal, rather than the quality of their work and the people who will pay for it. That is why they fail and will always fail.

Whenever I want to make more money, I don't focus on the money, but on my work. I try to find ways to improve the quality. And I have edited some of the most well-sold books many times. I have also republished my music after working on the equalization of the sounds in each one of them. And yet, a

UNCOMMON: TRANSCENDING THE LIES OF THE MENTAL HEALTH INDUSTRY

lot of my work does not produce the results I expect. I simply keep on being consistent with this principle, and that's why I am a successful full-time artist and author for nearly ten years.

Other people, the vast majority, can't see things from this angle. They obsess too much over the money part. And this is why, even though I wish I could share my life with a spouse, my relationships failed. Because, if people can't live without going to the beach for one weekend, if they can't stop being drunk all the time, if they can't say 'no' to a party, then they can't be part of my life, and likewise, when the time comes for me to spend a whole year in an island enjoying the sun, I have to do this part alone too.

As sad as it is to say, most people are just too stupid. Their misery is a consequence of their stupidity. But they are often stupid because they are greedy and lazy.

So should I feel pity for them? I feel pity for those who read a lot, work hard and can't achieve what they want. But I never found a single person who reads a lot and works a lot and can't get what they want.

As a matter of fact, I never met a person who works hard, reads many books on mental health, and suffers with mental problems. It doesn't happen! Because as soon as you become determined to solve your problems, you find the answers, you find the right people, and you do solve them.

The law of manifestation or attraction is real, you do attract that in which you are focused, but only if you are willing to work for it and are open to receive it.

This law applies to wealth as much as it applies to happiness and mental health. It is in the process that manifestation truly occurs.

Chapter 38: What are the Levels of Our Hierarchy of Needs?

Most people would say that they can't enjoy life without a plasma screen, a big car, and so on, but when having these things, they want more and bigger things.

This constant needing, like a parasite feeding on anxiety and depression, makes them miserable. And yet, they feel somehow comfortable in their life cycles.

Many europeans spend an entire year saving money to travel for fifteen days in Asia, and asians spend the entire year saving money to travel for fifteen days in Europe. Most people from the countryside feel bored with their life and want to travel to big cities to enjoy their time there. And those in such cities feel anxious and stressed with so much movement, and want to relax in the countryside. And so, something must be terribly wrong with the way we interpret life, because everyone seems confused about what they want and need, and how to satisfy such needs and wants.

The answer won't come without a proper introspection related to who we are. And this leads to another misunderstanding, which is that they must be appreciated and love before they can appreciate and love themselves.

The conflicting behaviors trap too many people in a paradox that makes no sense. Their emotions tell them exactly that. But loving yourself is about doing and being what makes you respect yourself.

For example,...

- If a person says, "I'm not beautiful enough", the answer is: "Make yourself look beautiful!"

- If she says "I don't have enough money", the answer is: "Search for cheaper clothes of quality that make you feel better!"

- For "I am not confident enough", the answer is: "Listen to music that makes you feel good, and relax in a park, listen to the birds singing, and try to meet new people!"

- And finally, it the person says, "I don't have enough friends to go out", the answer is: "Join clubs, associations, sports activities, and so on, until you have enough friends!"

Most people are so immersed in their thinking patterns that they can't see these possibilities I mentioned, and often create barriers for themselves, before even trying.

The capacity to self-love is the first and most important step in healing, and we can help another person by inviting him or her out to do things that can bring them joy. A walk in the park can make miracles for the most depressive person, and also sunshine and a walk on the beach.

As the person feels more confident and self-reliable with the activities, it is possible to develop a better self-esteem and self-respect, which will be the second and third steps in the recovery process.

Whenever someone mutilates her body in some way, that person is showing a need to be validated, and appreciated. The person as decreased in her needs from respect to validation. And in fact, social media has, to a large extent, made people succumb to simpler forms of validation.

If we have to draw a pyramid of what would be normal, we would have the following, starting from the top:

- Level one — The need to be seen as an influential element of society;

- Level two — The need to be respected by society;

- Level three — The need to be part of society;

- Level four — The need to contribute to society;

UNCOMMON: TRANSCENDING THE LIES OF THE MENTAL HEALTH INDUSTRY

- Level five — The need to be seen by society;
- Level six — The need to exist.

What is wrong in the world of today, is that people want to be at level one as artists and musicians, and at level two as important business owners, but spend most of their time at level five and six.

They do this by taking too many photos of themselves, spending too much time on social media, and trying to make their appearance noticeable by others. As a result, they get further and further from what they want in life.

Then, comes the false sense of entitlement, the belief that one has the right to a job and a good salary, and a family, which would be level three and four. Except that such individuals lack the social skills to be able to interact with the rest of society at a healthy level.

When these persons finally recognize they have a problem, they don't even realize what the problem is. They are too much within the sixth level — inexistence.

They want their therapist to tell them who they are. And that's what they spend the next months talking about. But while a good therapist would try to make the patient understand his personality, at this state, the patient is seeking mostly validation and attention. And that's why both get nowhere.

Does the therapist care? No! He is being paid!

Does the patient care? No! He is being validated!

Most people actually say about their psychologists: "It's great to have someone with whom you can talk openly."

That resumes the failure of therapy. Which could be corrected if every therapist has a supervisor to whom they would have to explain their failures.

They don't! It's an arbitrary process.

The fact that both therapist and patient are comfortable with the situation, despite not producing any results, doesn't mean the process is going well.

An angry reaction is common when we realize that we have been wrong for many years. And it is better to be angry than to be depressed. Anger always follows a state of depression and it is natural — it is the awareness of a need for self-validation.

The problem only exists when this need is sought from the outside, as when people put efforts to be accepted by others, as it may not always happen.

Chapter 39: How Does Mental Illness Affect Behavior?

If we need to seek a way outside of us to balance the inside, then the activities that bridge the gap better are those who allow some form of direct contact with our inner alchemy, such as sports and meditation.

A simple bicycle ride, for example, can help in alleviating depression. The routine then helps in shifting our physical state to a new one. But a similar outcome can be obtained with our diet.

Ultimately, we want to keep ourselves active with the right elements. For it is the combination of action with chemistry that improves our overall mental health.

Even if we need to address our thoughts, we know that it is difficult to think when we are doing an exhausting physical activity. But we also know that we think more clearly afterwards. And so, we can assume that the only therapies that produce results, even if we are talking about hypnosis, are those which recreate the balance that the individual is seeking towards a goal.

No matter how crazy the life of someone may seem, the individual heals through action. And we have the artists as an example. Their art is who they are, and when they are producing art, they are understanding themselves. That act of expressing oneself, is a metacognitive process that allows to see oneself too.

Now, the question is, how do we make someone who is mentally ill want to move and do something? Isn't that a contradiction to their state?

I would say that it is a contradiction as much as expecting them to talk.

Moving them to a park can produce more results than closing such individuals within four walls and expecting some results from the therapeutical process. The individual doesn't really heal when mirroring himself and his condition, but when he understands the correlation between himself and the world.

His relationship with his mother doesn't matter, unless he can see how he produces the same thoughts and emotions towards other women. And the same applies to women and their relationship with their father.

Certainly, every case is different, but it is in this correlation of past and present that we truly see the benefits of any therapy.

If you hypnotize someone without this in mind, you will drive the individual insane. But an hypnosis that doesn't address introspection is equally dangerous.

One of the problems with people who are depressed, for example, is that they very easily adapt to negative cycles, habits and routines. They even become obsessed with that as a way to escape any introspection.

As an example, someone who is suffering from depression due to unemployment, will obsess over getting a job, and won't have the clarity of mind to try to improve her curriculum. She will also try to get a job out of fear, rather than genuine interest in the interviewer and what he does. And with such behaviors, the person actually drifts apart furthermore from getting any offer.

The more dependent people are on their salary, the more incapacitate they will be, mentally and emotionally, to solve a problem related to it. The solution is then to give them something that they can feel safe with. But what can that be?

Quite honestly, there is nothing that can replace money, except gold and possessions.

If one is afraid to be poor, that will certainly drive him or her insane. And there is a correlation between poor mental health and homelessness for this reason. The social image of the individual, and his as a result, are compromised.

Solidarity and friendships that are supportive would prevent such descent but most people don't help their friends when they're in need. And that's the real problem here.

Mental health is a problem of society as a whole. And when this society fails the individual, he doesn't have many other alternatives, if any.

Chapter 40: Why is Mental Health a Social Problem?

A person has to somehow learn to be hopeless and self-reliable to overcome his situation, and most are not.

The only situations known in which someone was self-reliable in a situation of poverty and overcome it, is related to those who had religious beliefs.

We can therefore claim that religion fulfills the gap that society doesn't. But there are other ways. And someone who is unemployed, even if receiving benefits from the government, or being supported by friends and relatives, should, at the very least, do some type of volunteering or internship in a company, to build character and increase the levels of motivation. Because, as it was mentioned, it is the correlation with the outside through certain practices that improves mental health.

Any mental patient who is occupied with an activity that benefits someone, or even animals and nature, his working towards a better state of mind, with more clarity and self-esteem. Even gardening can match what I am saying here.

I do recommend gardening and some type of work with animals for those who suffer with psychopathy and in particular, narcissists.

As a matter of fact, saying in a job interview that you have done some volunteering will increase your chances to get the job, as well as the trust of others on your commitment to fulfill a certain agreement. You automatically become more trustworthy as a person. And society can only work based on trust and compromises.

That notion, will certainly make you feel healthier and act in healthier ways.

As an example, an economic crisis isn't really a crisis in itself except when it disrupts a previously functional system. And those who depended on that system will certainly contribute to the crisis. But those who did not depend on it, will survive it. And those who were above the crisis, will benefit from it.

What I am saying is that small business owners who profited from the actions and habits of the majority, such as restaurant owners, are the first to go. But investors and entrepreneurs, if they think out of the herd mentality, can always see a way to make their business survive or prosper in such moments. The one who has an independent mind, actually tends to do better in a crisis. Because while others are shaken by the storms, he is moving faster, as if the weight of society was lifted from him.

My best time ever as an author, for example, was during the COVID19 pandemic. My profits tripled in just two months. Because people were bored, unemployed, and with nothing useful to do, they started reading more. But they didn't read anything. They chose to read the authors they trusted. These were the ones profiting the most.

You can't really do anything without trust. Not as a job seeker and not as an artist.

This is something that most artists fail to understand when quitting their jobs to pursue a full-time career as an artist. The level of commitment necessary is higher and the principles of hard work and trust between themselves and others still applies. You can't just do whatever you want, if you want to get rich.

The art of getting rich actually consists in doing what you must within the reality in front of you. And the same applies to mental health. You can be uncommon to a certain extent, before you are labeled as a freak of society. You can be different to the extent that you can keep a small circle of people around you, but not so eccentric that you find yourself completely isolated.

There is only a crisis for those that weren't ready for it. In economy as in life, to be prepared is the best vaccine or drug to deal with a depression.

Chapter 41: Can Depression Prevent You From Achieving Goals?

We can see now that depression represents a biological alarm for not having a life matching our emotional requirements. The bigger the gap, the loudest the alarm sounds.

The biggest problem of the educational system then becomes the fact that it keeps training individuals for a world that doesn't exist, while not providing the necessary tools to allow a psychological and emotional preparation for an unpredictable future.

The individual is trained, fundamentally, to be dependent and helpless on his own.

If we fear independent thinkers, we will inevitably have more people suffering from mental illness. Because there is correlation between the lack of imagination and creativity in society and mental illness.

On the other hand, one cannot help himself without creating a revolution within his personality, and which invariably represents a revolution towards the outside world.

The more the world tries to unify itself under invariable premises, to avoid dissents, the more those dissent will appear in the form of individuals who suffer from depression and psychopathy.

Narcissism, or the obsessive need for social validation, is a symptom of the lack of opportunities and options. Even more so, when that becomes a lifestyle and way of living.

The models on social media are certainly the ones more at risk from suffering an emotional breakdown and ending with a very bad depression.

People ignore them and laugh when such individuals cry on camera, because they do not understand how strong is the impact of social media on one's mind and emotions.

The more we depend on social media, the more we lose our independent capacity to think effectively.

Social media should be a tool, but sadly, it is not. It is another mechanism of control. The more one uses this tool, the more he himself becomes as a tool.

Any activity that robs you from the act of thinking independently and make your own conclusions, is bad for your mental health.

Education can be as bad as social media, or watching television, even though these activities seem harmless.

The opposite of this would be to be able to built your own house in a land you own.

That is why such was so important for the first pilgrims who arrived in the United States. These desperate people understood the importance of being independent and free from any system, far before it starts to oppress them.

If we want to promote mental health, we need to stimulate creativity, work, independent thinking and freedom.

No therapy will ever work, except through luck, if not following these principles.

Only then, having a life purpose makes more sense, as a way to motivate us in our journey. But a good life purpose shouldn't be unrealistic. Should make sense to the individual.

This said, I must stress the incongruence I notice in those who take psychotropic drugs but have high goals, such as becoming entrepreneurs or writers. For these goals have more to do with their self-esteem and ego than reality itself. And because they are more likely to fail, these become dangerous goals to have. But does this mean they should not have these goals?

Not necessarily! But, in one cause I know personally, he has been taking antidepressants for as long as a he wants to become a rich business owner. And twenty years have passed since.

UNCOMMON: TRANSCENDING THE LIES OF THE MENTAL HEALTH INDUSTRY

It is obvious that he will never make it. But I am not being pessimistic. I am looking at the facts.

I tried to help this friend by telling him that I knew factories in China that could produce for him. He refused, saying that it was too far. Then I tried to help him build a e-commerce website. And he refused too, claiming that I just wanted his money.

In other words, he is too stupid, due to the many years of repeated failures, to accomplish his goals. He never will!

If this person accepted help from someone who knows more than him, either me or someone else, he could succeed. But the problem with an extended amount of failures, is that the individual becomes absorbed in his own imaginary world. He has disconnected himself from the outside world for too long, and everything in his reality is now part of a vast amount of habits and thoughts that reinforce his imaginary but unrealistic version of himself.

You see, the difference between a person like this and a successful entrepreneur, is that the successful entrepreneur owns his mistakes, learns from his mistakes and moves on with such lessons in mind. Successful business owners fail before they succeed, because they are learning from their own failures. But the mentally ill person can't do that! This person will detach himself from his own results.

In all the cases of mentally ill individuals, we see the same. Whenever someone attempts to justify his own actions and shift responsibility to someone else, he has started a downward path towards insanity.

There is a joke about this topic, in which two prisoners find themselves in a cell having a conversation about their background:

— "Why are you in jail?", Asks one.

— "Because the police caught me", Says the other.

The less responsibility one has and the less able the person is to confront his own mistakes and problems, the more likely he is to fail and to be or keep being mentally ill.

The personality cannot shift on its own. And the fact that this friend of my story keeps going to psychiatrists for all these years, shows me that he is communicating with morons that don't know anything about mental health, and just want to make a profit out of him, which is actually the case with the mental industry in general.

You can't cure anyone unless you make him own his behaviors and the consequences of such behaviors.

It is interesting to notice, however, that many violent criminals and psychopaths, only seem to get enlightened about what they did when they are about to be put to death. Ted Bundy did a brilliant interview just hours before being executed. Almost didn't seem the same person who proudly murdered women, almost didn't seem like a dangerous psychopath.

Fear is a powerful mechanism of control in society, but if that is all we have, then the overall moral of a people will always be low, as in "the fear of being caught".

Chapter 42: What are The Benefits of Using Your Imagination?

Imagination is the ultimate frontier between mind and reality, but not a bad one. Our imagination operates as an emotional compensation, to avoid confronting an emotionally painful reality.

I used to be a daydreamer when I was in school and throughout my entire school life. And the teachers told my parents that even though I was smart, the fact I couldn't pay attention, was the cause of my bad grades.

That was true but only at a superficial level. I was daydreaming because I was extremely depressed, and I was very depressed because I was raised by two morons — two narcissistic and very mentally sick individuals that kept insulting me and downgrading me. Daydreaming was how my mind protected itself. But it certainly didn't help when I started getting bullied too, for being different, maladapted.

The whole society blames you, and never itself, when you are suffering.

I was basically, being discriminated, for not paying attention, for having no self-esteem and for being humiliated at home.

Which chance did I have? None! I was doomed to be mentally ill, drugged, and maybe commit suicide.

What saved me was a combination of miracles, that most people in the same situation, simple don't have.

What my parents and teachers saw as a schizophrenia developing, was actually my telepathic communication with the spiritual world improving. I was being helped, and because that help was producing results, and was a positive help, I took it.

During all of my life, I have always been in different religious groups, and had learned to pray there. I also learned quite a lot about meditation and the spiritual world with those people. That is why I was developing such skills.

It certainly helped that I had the habit of meditating three times a day, for one hour each time, since I was 12yo. For as my abilities developed, I was eventually catapulted out of that reality. My grades improved so much, nobody could believe.

I remember a conversation I once had with a psychologist in the school, who told me:

— "You know you are not like others! You are special!"

I started to laugh. Because I didn't really care about what she believed. I had nothing else to learn at that point. By the time I was 16yo, I had already devoured entire encyclopedias on mental health, psychiatry, and so on.

I was fully aware and in control of my life. Telling me that I was special, produced no effect in me. Not at that point! My self-esteem was already high enough, I had moved from being unpopular to being popular. From being bullied to winning fights. From being ridiculed by women to being able to get an attractive girlfriend.

When she saw that I felt contempt for her knowledge, she told me to leave the room.

I still have contempt for psychologists in general, but is not a personal thing. I simply despise their arrogance, which is rooted on a fantasy. Psychology helps nobody.

Psychology couldn't certainly help me. But that experience wasn't enough. I eventually volunteered to help children with learning disabilities, and was successful with all of them, because I had mastered the art of controlling the mind better than psychologists.

They could not help those same children!

I am not saying, however, that I am important. And this is something that I was able to make the children understand but adults couldn't. It is the ability to accept help, that is the real miracle, and not the person.

UNCOMMON: TRANSCENDING THE LIES OF THE MENTAL HEALTH INDUSTRY

Many times, countless teachers and psychologists, tried to rob my techniques with those children, to promote themselves as more capacitated than me, and felt frustrated and angry for not being able to do it. And sadly, they represent a majority of the society, always trying to rob everyone from their knowledge, but not truly invested in helping.

I have seen teachers and politicians teaching what I developed on camera, but none ever asked me to talk on camera. And this obsession people have with their own ego, makes me feel sick. That is why I stopped helping others in this field.

There is indeed a correlation between our mental issues and the sickness of our society. That was part of my own learning too. I had to overcome that as well. Nevertheless, now that I am 40yo, I still have morons asking me questions about the type of relationship I have with my parents. Even women judge me in such a way. And that goes to show you why most people are so mentally ill.

You cannot trust anyone who is emotionally codependent on his family. That person will never be a sane individual, even if appearing to be one. You only have to squeeze him or her a little more to see what I am saying, for such person can't make proper independent decisions.

Chapter 43: How Setting Goals Can Help Your Mental Health?

Our dreams, either related to the future, or simply fantasies about our reality, maintain a certain equilibrium that is necessary for our sanity.

Narcissists typically have many nightmares because they lie a lot. Liars can't have much of a sanity, because they are constantly trying to coordinate facts with fiction.

On the other hand, just as with our night dreams, our day dreams must necessarily follow a correlation to how our mind is operating, therefore the importance of analyzing them under that light.

If one feels undeserving of life, dreams may reflect that, by becoming nightmares that reflect an obsession with death and suffering. But there is certainly a personality within the dream, even if the dream appears to be absurd.

The dreams we have at night can't take us very far, except towards explaining the subconscious of the individual. But the day dreams can help us find the cure to such individual. If we are able to break the dream of the person in smaller but easily measurable steps, we can help this person find her cure on her own.

I have found that, instinctively, everyone is wanting to cure themselves.

It is interesting, for example, that many narcissists I met, show a strong interest in having a pet and in volunteering with children and homeless people. They somehow know that their need for validation is a sickness, which, on the other hand, comes from lack of empathy.

By working with vulnerable people who need compassion and empathy, they get that validation they need in a healthy way, while also working through their own mental illness and towards the cure.

We can then assume that the worse mistakes therapists do, in any case, is to believe that the patient needs to be analyzed and judged, or evaluated, more than understood. Or that the patient, himself, doesn't know how to find his own cure.

I would never understand so much about how to cure narcissism and psychopathy, if I did not observed how such individuals are already trying to cure themselves.

They fail, simply, because the majority of society does not help them, but rather pushes them further to their death.

Whenever people tell their friends: "If your relationship doesn't work, find someone else", They are teaching the individual to escape responsibility. And people constantly say these things to each other, because the majority of society truly believe in these behaviors, the majority is very and horribly mentally sick.

In the past, that wouldn't be what you would hear. Society was constantly putting efforts to sustain itself, and understand itself. Divorce wasn't so common.

We can discuss how good or bad that was, but what we can't deny is that, as soon as you remove responsibility from a person, you condemn that person to insanity. Because she will fail, again and again. And in time, she will be less able to introspect and take responsibility for her actions.

Trying to help a woman in her early 20s is not the same as trying to help her in her 40s. You can hardly rehabilitate an individual that spent a lifetime running from problems.

The steps to do it, are, nonetheless, the same in any situation: You make the person take responsibility and act towards learning from her own behaviors.

If a woman complains about violent men, for example, then she certainly needs to accept the fact that she is attracted to psychopaths. A fact, by the way, which has been proven by science.

UNCOMMON: TRANSCENDING THE LIES OF THE MENTAL HEALTH INDUSTRY

Women are commonly attracted to men who show psychopathic traits. But a man who is attracted to overly dramatizing women, on the other hand, is one that lacks self-esteem. And again, we see this in many studies too.

The benefits that women now receive, made men obsolete as a gender. To compete with women, they have to somehow abdicate of their self-esteem.

That is more prominent in the workplace, because men lack the mental skills that women naturally have, when dealing with social environments.

Whatsoever is the case, overcoming depression, requires finding a way of gaining more control over life while seeking expectable results. Within this strategy, we'll encounter the need to teach self-respect and responsibility to someone who keeps finding ways to sabotage his own results, namely by refusing to follow the opportunities that life offers him or her.

These small steps in-between goals will reinforce habits which conduct to self-esteem and, eventually, achievement as well.

If a patient needs to take guitar lessons to arrive to the goal of becoming a musician, for example, he will need to conduct a certain amount of tasks, often neglected due to depression, such as taking a shower, going out of the house, having lunch, taking a walk in the street, being in public, meeting new people, before he can have his classes. And that cycle of habits can indeed rehabilitate the person.

A life purpose isn't as important as cycles of action that the person is willing to take to get it.

Chapter 44: Why Do We Try to Fit in?

Those that complain about their past, aren't usually willing to change their future, either because they think they can't or because they think that they don't deserve that future.

This mindset is related to a period in time, either past, present or future, and their behavior follows accordingly. And so, as simple as it may seem, the communication with such individuals, to be effective, must inject the component of "possibility" in the individual, before he can develop his own immunology against abasement, apathy and low self-esteem.

You should be able, for example, to show where someone who is losing in life, has won before. And show to someone suffering with depression, when, in the past, that person was able to feel happy.

This shift of mental observation increases the motivation and self-esteem, because we all want to succeed, and we all can fail, but those who keep themselves permanently in depression are attached to their failures, more than the prospect of succeeding.

Someone with a positive mindset, will spend most of the time looking at his achievements and the potential for more achievements, while someone depressed spends most of the time looking at his own failures. The difference, we can say, is related to faith, at least in oneself, if not in an external figure, such as God.

The problem with a low self-esteem is in essence a problem of lack of faith, in oneself or God.

We can then see that life can only be evaluated based on how we perceive it to be and not what it is.

I may get many of my friends sending me messages when one of my book reaches the best selling charts of Amazon, but they didn't help me write it, many of them where not next to me when I wrote, they did not motivate me to write it, they did not told me I could write a good book, they did not help me edit it, and so on. They were never in any of the steps of the process. From the idea, to be belief I could do it, to the time invested, and the words written, it was all and only done by me alone.

As I have found, both mental health and success are then correlated between one another and relative to the importance we give to society. The more you care about "fitting in" and "pleasing others", the more likely you are to never accomplish anything interesting enough to move you upwards to the first positions as an artist, a successful entrepreneur or a writer.

I have succeeded in many areas of life, and have helped many people succeed too, in music, in writing, in education with both students and teachers, in theatre, in public speaking, in business, and so on. And what I saw, was always the same: Those who are too obsessed with what others think of them are lost cases. A successful mindset doesn't care about that!

I always see my results as a natural consequence of my work. And so, when someone says "Congratulations", it means nothing to me, unless this person was next to me during the production stage and somehow encouraged me.

As you can imagine, this applies perfectly well to relationships and even nations. If I am working very hard in the mist of disrespectful morons, as is the case of the Portuguese, the Spaniards, the Lithuanians or the Polish, I will certainly not remain too long in the country. And yet, whenever I arrive in any nation, the question everyone asks is: "How long will you stay?"

You see, they are too stupid to see that the question in itself is wrong. And so, they don't understand when I answer: "I don't know!"

I obviously don't know because I only make a decision to stay longer in a country if I see that country adjusting to my will and not the opposite. But because the majority always wants to fit in, they get stupider by default. They sacrifice their dreams to the god of "fitting in" and as a result of their stupid efforts, they get stupid prizes — failures, frustration and depression.

It is certainly difficult to have the right mindset in a world full of morons. But that's how I succeed. That's the secret to success.

UNCOMMON: TRANSCENDING THE LIES OF THE MENTAL HEALTH INDUSTRY

Now, as a result of such attitude, people will hate you too. Because, you see, as they are obsessed with fitting in and acting like a sheep, they think you are the one in the wrong for not doing it. They will see you as an outcast, a criminal, a rebel, an antisocial personality.

That, I must say, is the price you pay for being mentally sane amidst the deeply insane.

Once you become uncommonly healthy, you become a target for the commonly unhealthy.

Like a disease, they will try to eliminate you and self-destroy themselves. That's what infected human beings do! They act like they are diseases.

The zombies are all around you — they are the many people infected with a herd mentality keeping them stupid. That infection comes from fitting in.

You don't fit in with the crazies! You don't fit in among crocodiles and snakes! You don't fit in with infected people! That's the stupidest thing you can do.

Just imagine a monkey going to a therapist because the crocodiles want to eat him. The monkey shouldn't have to even consider fitting in with the crocodiles. That's not how nature and logic works.

Chapter 45: Can Discrimination Be Harmful to Your Mental Health?

A person in apathy has simply given up in trying to understand life and others, and that's when suicide becomes the most obvious solution, even though not being more than a way out when no other is found.

The reason why Lithuanians all kill themselves, and Lithuania, despite being a tiny insignificant country, is number one world in suicide, is because that whole nation is sick. And the fact that they keep blaming the Soviet Union for it, proves, as this book has shown you, that they will never reach the level of responsibility necessary to heal.

The Lithuanians are xenophobic because they are deeply insane. And you can't cure a nation without destroying it first as one.

If we organized nations according to the mental health of the population, we would know that nations that can't take responsibility for their development and accept the help of immigrants, shouldn't have the right to be nations. They should be forced to merge with neighboring nations and disappear as one. But people don't like to hear this! Because they have this imbecile neurosis called "national pride".

If you can't choose where your passport is made, having national pride is delusional and ridiculous.

I hope it doesn't take 10 thousand years into the future, for this planet to realize it.

If you care about your mental health, you should be able to see it. Because, you can improve your mental health by just changing borders.

I have seen many who improved themselves by simply doing this.

There is nothing wrong with abandoning the country where you were born if it's sick and keeping you from evolving and becoming healthier and happier.

Our attitude to life and our surroundings can and will determine our whole future.

For example, in two real life situations, I noticed that individuals with the same life purpose reacted differently to similar experiences. A woman who wrote a book, when she was a teenager, showed it to a teacher who criticized her, and so she burned the manuscript and never wrote again. In another case, a man was told by a psychologist that his IQ was below the average and he shouldn't even try to go to university, but he refused to accept this judgment and fifteen years later became a professor in not one, but several universities, and published more than one hundred bestsellers.

That woman was one of my former girlfriends, and that man is me. The difference between these two person is related to the amount of self-esteem they have.

Our self-esteem determines our success in life as well as our happiness. But we tend to make so many efforts to please others and be part of society that, in the end, we forget the fact that we can't be loved without loving ourselves first.

Before paying attention to what others want, you should be aware of what you want. Quite often, you owe no explanations to anyone.

Our personality and social identity are two different things, being the first related to thinking patterns we develop in life according to the second. We shouldn't let the second affect the first. Our priority is our well-being and development, and not the well-being of others according to us.

That is not being selfish but responsible! Your life belongs to you only!

In fact, the problem that a pandemic creates is exactly a moral problem. Should everyone be vaccinated because some got infected? If vaccines truly worked, that wouldn't be necessary. But this idea that everyone must be vaccinated against some disease, shows us that people are too stupid to realize that vaccines don't work. They are too obsessed with controlling the life of others to realize this obvious fact.

UNCOMMON: TRANSCENDING THE LIES OF THE MENTAL HEALTH INDUSTRY

Most people have such strong thinking patterns, that they can't rationalize outside of their own paradigms. They actually reinforce them with others who think the same. That's why you can have an entire university acting in the same imbecile way, or doctors from all over the planet following the same dumb procedures.

A large amount of morons doesn't make them correct because of their numbers. But this is why you need to first and necessarily become uncommon, before you can reeducate yourself.

This reeducation is a shift of paradigms based on self-learning.

Then, and only then, you will understand happiness as it is for you, and not as you were told to believe.

Healing the mind is a path of rediscovery. But, when changing, nothing about you is lost, only parts of what you aren't as an individual may be lost. Your true identity is never forgotten and can't be detached from your real self.

If you can love life and yourself, you can't be depressed, because you are in harmony with your real self. And so, a change is always made inwards for it to succeed.

In order to change effectively, a person needs to pragmatically and critically apply the use of intelligence, by comparing similarities and differences in life's given situations, by measuring possible outcomes and always choose the most positive ones, and so on.

A simple exercise in this direction, consists of comparing friends who uplift you with those who suppress you. For the key to significant changes consists in following the most positive decisions in life.

Most people don't know how to judge what is good or bad, and so they fear changing, as they believe that the good can become bad and the bad may or may not become good. That's when phrases like "to do mistakes is human" or "suffering is part of life" come into place. This is what people assume in order to refuse any change. But the problem with negativity is that it leads nowhere, while positive perspectives promote change, as they're related to understanding and assimilating our own results.

It is easy to change when you can see that you're moving towards a better reality. If you don't fear life, you can't fear change.

Chapter 46: Why Do We Feel Rejected?

As many statistics show, the vast majority of the population suffers from mental problems and has an IQ below normal levels. This means they are both stupid and mentally sick.

We shouldn't be surprised then that they behave in antisocial manners or look at others passing by in the street as if they were afraid to be infected by some contagious virus.

The way people look at others is a sign of their mental illness. Let us not get this confused.

When we talk about the majority we are not necessarily talking about human beings, but about a bunch of neurotics and psychopaths walking around, pretending to be civilized.

When we are trying to be different, and improve ourselves, we have to necessarily deal with that dysfunctional majority.

These same sick individuals, secretly wish everyone was sick like them. That way, they wouldn't be pointed out and identified as a threat to society. And because they are majority, quite many of the problems we have to deal with in this world, either related to lies, provocations, disrespect, racism and xenophobia, is related to such persons.

We end up getting involved in many arguments with people that, quite honestly, can't even think properly. But we also attract them to our life because we don't discriminate them.

Discrimination is indeed necessary as part of the process of being mentally sane. It has to simply be applied properly.

On the other hand, the sense of belonging has to be relativized. Not feeling part of a group of sick people, for example, would be something to be proud about, and a very healthy behavior. Not feeling understood by the stupid and the moronic sheep of society, as well.

It is said that being a leader is an isolating process. But the same applies to being mentally sane. Whenever you act better than the majority, you risk some form of segregation. Because humans have a tendency to project their mental issues rather than introspect them.

The insane attack the sane the most, as much as the ugly hate the beautiful, and the dumb tend to hate the smart, and the poor hate the rich.

Many times I don't even have any clue as to why someone hates me, because the reasons I end up finding are too stupid for me to even consider. Some hate me because I am smarter than them, others because I am richer, others because I don't need a job and they do, others because I am more successful than them.

People always hate you for reflecting back at them their own problems, even when you are doing that unintentionally, just by being yourself.

As you become a better version of what a human must be, the more this is likely to happen. Because you may end up reflecting the problems of the vast majority.

I have been hated all my life for different reasons, and I will continue to be hated for the rest of my life for other reasons.

The losers of society, which are a vast majority, and the imbeciles, which are a vast majority too, will always hate those who are far ahead of them. That's why they are losers, they can't learn and assimilate their problems. They feel entitled and think the world owes them something. They have no consideration or respect for the background of others who worked much harder than they ever will.

The vast majority of the people are attached to their family because they are insecure and afraid to step out of their comfort zone.

The problem with feeling comfort with a dysfunctional family, is that the individual will then seek to replicate this drama in other environments, even when finding a healthy and patient partner. If someone spent a great portion of her life witnessing drama and suffering, she will not feel familiar with the emotions of love and affection.

Chapter 47: Why Do We Feel Lonely?

The need to belong is normal but, eventually, you will have to learn to make decisions. Just because you belong to a group of people, doesn't mean it's the right group for you. Our friends rarely have our best interests in sight, but always their own. And we always become as those we spend most of our time with. We merge our thoughts, values and aspirations, or expectations, with theirs, both consciously and subconsciously.

You always need a certain dose of self-control around people, but it is always better to feel relaxed around those you admire and love. However, you should remember you won't ever be accepted by everyone, and even those who accept you today, may change tomorrow, and start seeing you differently.

Respect is a thin line that many tend to cross, but necessary, towards ourselves and others, if we wish to be free to evolve independently, as we allow others to do the same.

Many years ago, after I moved to China for work, a friend confessed to me that he admired me. But then, as he was living a horrible life, feeling miserable and taking pills for depression, and was even unable to find a spouse to get married, he started hating me. That hate came both as a sense of jealousy and frustration.

The same happened to another friend, who was find with my personality when assuming that his life was better than mine. He had inherited a fortune from his father, while I was always working hard for my results. But when he saw that my life had improved, and I then had a beautiful girlfriend, while he was single, he couldn't live with that. He told me that he wanted to meet her, but only because he expected her to be unattractive, and not the type of woman that often rejects him.

He stopped talking to me after that day!

Those two friends had changed, even if I knew them for many years, but the changes where predictable. People are jealous, and have low self-esteem. Most of what they tell us comes from that mindset.

Even when your life improves in a natural way, most people will not accept that. Many other friends, for example, insulted me when they found I was rich. Because they have seen me working very hard for many years, but never imagined I could have results from all that work. They still don't believe! Now, they think I'm a criminal and avoid me.

All the people you know, believe in what they see and think of you. As you change, you will find it hard to have them adapt to those changes.

Should we adapt to others?

That's a question that some people answer as yes and others as no.

You see, to be fully honest here, nobody is really your friend. They are just friends to the image they possess of you. Therefore, friendships tend to be relative to how people feel about such image, and which always reflects them. And so, the friendship emerges from a relationship with their ego.

Basically, even if I don't intend to hurt my male friends, they will always compete with me, and feel inferior if losing that competition.

As for the female friends, they will always feel either attraction or despise, and can't just maintain the friendship at a normal ground.

The very few who can adapt to your changes, either men or women, are, in general, one in ever 100 you meet. Which means you need to meet a thousand people to make 10 reliable friends. But even among these, I have come to realize that the ones who keep contact with me, as I travel a lot, are those who somehow need me.

These tend to disappear when they meet someone else with your qualities, talents or knowledge.

Whenever I met individuals who seem to have many friends, I noticed that all practice what I call "tribalism". They close themselves in their group of shared values, often a religion or some group with common goals, like those who gather to play games or go to parties. They do expand their friendships and social life, but within a predetermined circle of common interests.

UNCOMMON: TRANSCENDING THE LIES OF THE MENTAL HEALTH INDUSTRY

Not many people are willing to talk to strangers and make new friendships. It requires too many efforts and is seen as a risky activity. But how can one grow and evolve, if he fears losing his group of friends?

I have always been quick to lose all of my many friendships. I only had to disagree on them on fundamental values for that to happen, even if not interfering with their right to believe in whatever they want. Because groups depend on those values to exist, even if such values are dumb and stupid.

That is why it's hard to be constantly evolving and have many friends.

I have had many moments of my life in which I had hundreds or even thousands of friendships, that soon after vanished. Because I evolve and change extremely fast, and most people can't handle that.

When I was working in music, I knew famous DJs, club owners, event management companies, and had a huge list of followers, over seven thousand. They all vanished when I said I would quit music to dedicate myself to writing books. Suddenly, I was nobody to them.

I have also seen this occurring with religious groups, political groups, and associations.

Many would say that such people are superficial, self-centered and short-minded. Yes, they are! But most people are superficial, self-centered and short-minded.

The only thing we can change about it is ourselves. I learned to accept this fact, even if it can be very painful every time I have to restart my life without friends, simply because I travel a lot and change extremely fast for a common human being.

That's why I am not a common human being.

However, to accept myself, I have to accept others. That's the only way to keep evolving and not judging the ones who eventually abandon me.

Most people are actually very lonely, but because of their low evolutionary state of mind, they can't see it.

The tribalistic sense of belonging is actually a sign of such low state of mind. Most people have a strong need to belong to a tribe. And even though many scientists would say that this is natural for a human being, it wouldn't be if the human race on this planet was more evolved. Because, from the psychological point of view, it is as if technology and society, as a system, had advanced in time, but humans remained stuck to their caveman brain.

Chapter 48: Why Loneliness Can Make You Successful?

If I hadn't choose loneliness in several moments of my life, I wouldn't have change enough to get the opportunities that I truly wanted for myself, despite what others thought that I should or could get or not. This attitude has its price!

When I begun isolating myself in school to study harder, I started getting bullied, as I didn't have friends around me to protect me anymore. The same happened later in life when I was focusing more on the results of the companies that employed me than the conversations and rumors between employees. I eventually realized that, working too hard made me isolated. Most people don't care about working! They care about their reputation only.

Our fear of loneliness and the feeling of despair when we're alone, is then explained by this irrational fear of death. Or is it rational? Because if most people are irrational, then the one who considers their irrationality must be rational himself.

We fear loneliness because it makes us feel in danger, unprotected and vulnerable. That is why loneliness leads to despair, anxiety, stress and depression too. It is not just a primitive predisposition because society isn't social. The social system in which we live is simply a layer covering the truth most of us experience almost on a daily basis.

Some cultures are more evolved than others, but most cultures are not evolved enough for sure. And there is a lot of poverty in this world, adding to these fears. Because people also know that poverty and isolation are related.

Could we then say that those who control the wealth of a people control their mental health? Certainly!

The way to solve this comes with an independent mindset, which that same majority attacks. Because they are so dependent on the system that the same fear they have of losing it, is the fear they reveal when someone abandons it. They protect the same system which they fear with an anger that is proportional to their fears.

This is why the nations with a longer history of poverty are so xenophobic.

At an individual level, we can even say that the stupider a person is, the more aggressive the behaviors will be towards that which he or she can't assimilate and comprehend. The fear of that which is different is more prominent in the stupid.

Which options the ones who are isolated then have?

When an elephant is abandoned by the group, he knows that it is just a matter of time before getting killed by a group of lions. And this is exactly what our instincts tell us about ourselves when we are segregated by society. We succumb to depression as if succumbing to our death.

In my personal life, and after changing to dozens of countries, and experiencing many different cultures, I came to the realization that I had no other choice but to build my own future. I became a more independent person, learned to accept this xenophobia and isolation towards which nearly all cultures condemned me, especially in Europe, and focused even more on my work.

As a result, I got richer and was able to enjoy a fulfilling life. But it was a life I could hardly match with anyone else. I became free from schedules and time and money problems, which others naturally cannot comprehend. And then I also noticed people were attracted to me due to these things that they wanted for themselves, rather than a genuine friendship, which contributed to make me selective for many years to come.

UNCOMMON: TRANSCENDING THE LIES OF THE MENTAL HEALTH INDUSTRY

Writing books became normal for me as the ideal path towards wealth, even though I have tried many others. In fact, I know that if I was born in France, I would probably become a musician instead. And maybe if I was born in the United States, I would have a great job in politics, and never care about writing books as well.

Somehow, the path that matches me the most, had to come from the same struggles that moved me apart from my background. That, however, makes me often think: Do we really have a choice in this life?

Our choices are so limited and so controlled by the society as a whole, that I don't think one really has a choice when trying to overcome depression, or even poverty.

Being abandoned by others and experiencing many years of loneliness, is quite often part of the process. And this emotional payment, that most people can't handle, is what makes entrepreneurs great.

Chapter 49: Why Do We Need Friends?

Too many people judge us for the amount of friends we have, as if that measured our value as human beings. But, you see, that's the path most choose for themselves too. That is why they use it as a reference for others. They think that their happiness and wealth depends on the quantity of friends they have. And then, their life, instead of being a road leading somewhere, becomes a cycle of stupidity in which they get comfortable. The years pass, and nothing happens, except drama and many bills to pay.

That cycle of home-office, office-home, pay this bill, pay that bill, deal with drama and fights, and rumors and jealousy, becomes their movie. Their life ends up becoming nothing more that some stupid Hollywood movie full of drama.

That, I must say, makes it impossible to go in the opposite direction. Because in all the relationships in which I was pulled backwards with all of this drama, I saw my dreams fading away in smoke. I was always angry, losing focus, and wasting my whole time in conversations and messages, that never truly resulted in anything different.

I had to end those relationships to get my life back, my dreams back.

A life without dreams is not worth living, but what if love stops those dreams? Will you choose love or the dreams?

After choosing love many times, I realized that following our dreams is better. Because love with drama, is a Mexican novel that never ends, except when you die. But dreams can lead to the manifestation of incredible things.

Ideally, we should have love and dreams combined. But when quite a lot of people are very stupid, you don't really get to choose.

One of the main problems with society, is that people believe they should have the right to do what they want. That is very dangerous for dumb people!

Freedom is for those who know what to do with it. Not for the stupid.

Whenever you give freedom to the stupid, you get more conflict, more wars, rape, murder, theft, and crime in general, and at all levels.

As soon as you notice that someone needs to lie too much, you must understand you are dealing with someone stupid. Because we shouldn't need to lie in a conversation. In fact, for as long as someone feels the need to lie about himself to others, he can't say those others are friends. The conversation isn't really happening. It seems rather like a game of spies.

We would think that inside universities the reality is different, but many years working as a college lecturer has showed me that it is not. At the college level, students are more indoctrinated, shaped to think in a certain way, but they still lack the same and fundamental knowledge as the masses, and that's why they are as stupid as anyone else.

Just because you learn how to think, that won't be useful if you don't possess the information that makes you think effectively.

This is something college graduates don't understand, because their purpose is to fit in into the highest section of society, and that's enough for their ego. They don't really, in many cases, have an independent personality of their own to consider what I just said. Those who do, quit their job to start something of their own, or never try to have one.

That is what I did, and that is why I spent the following years working from an apartment in front of the beach or in the city center of historical cities.

Unfortunately, most people aren't reasonable, even when they wear a uniform, and can't be argued with properly. They don't understand why they behave the way they do, and they don't care about knowing it or changing either. And so, respect has to be earned most of the times with the power of a fist or a weapon. That's why we still have wars and revolutions.

UNCOMMON: TRANSCENDING THE LIES OF THE MENTAL HEALTH INDUSTRY

There's this illusion that the world has become a better place to live since TV was invented, but it has actually become much worse. And that's why we need to be very selective about the people we surround ourselves with, even though, among more than 7 billion, there aren't actually many interesting or unique choices.

If you pay attention to groups of people talking, you will notice that, the bigger the group, the less meaningful is the conversation. Everything gets unreasonable and impersonal when the numbers increase.

For this reason, we can see how those who want many friends, also lose their personality in the process. It may be an emotional need that can be satisfied, but doesn't really built the personality. Not unless this group has an agenda of its own.

I'm very clear about the intentions of others, and that is why I know that having more friends isn't really the same as being more loved. This is an illusion most have. And, even though things could be different, the human race isn't ready for it, because most people don't really know how to love another being. Most people don't even know how to love themselves. Reason why psychotropics and marijuana sell more than books on confidence.

We can't expect from others things which they can't and won't ever give us. It's easier to find love within than outside of ourselves, and it's also easier to find people we can love than it is to expect love from those who don't love us.

Fundamentally, people become easily depressed because they can't live a lie and can't accept the truth. That's why antidepressants are so popular. If you can't live a lie and accept a truth, you can only be drugged. Reason why depression is called a mental illness, even though it is actually the inability to accept the problems of life and the fact that most people you love will may either despise you, hate you or abandon you.

I must say, nonetheless, that the greatest mental illness is to pretend that everything is fine with the world, but not with you, because the truth is exactly the opposite. The cure starts when you acknowledge this reality, rather than the one put before your eyes to blind you to the truth.

Chapter 50: How to Be a Better Person?

For reasons that escaped the awareness of most of us, happiness has turned into an abstract topic, something that seems difficult to acquire and understand, even relative to each person. It seems now that every and each individual has his or her own concept of happiness. But is it truly relative?

Most experts claim that happiness depends on the personality of each individual, on our values and needs, and yet, we ignore the fundamental principles behind being a happy person, and which are related to how we connect to the rest of the world — how we socialize.

Moreover, if we aren't making efforts towards increasing and strengthening such connections, we're neglecting as well the elements that make them possible, and which are part of the whole paradigm regarding what makes us feel alive and truly grateful for being alive.

Most got used to the idea that life is about struggles, challenges and suffering, but it is not. We weren't meant to live a whole experience of struggles and pains. On the contrary, we were born to be happy, spread happiness and fulfill the desires of our soul, the ambitions of our spirit and the needs of our mind. We were born to be altruistic in our actions and humanitarian in our thoughts.

Affinity composes the emotional side of a person but any emotion is fundamentally rooted in experience, in a reality that was felt by the individual, even though reality is determined by the level of attachment and agreements of the individual.

If I have to talk to someone I don't like, experience a daily job with individuals that make me unhappy, that will definitely contribute to a lower sense of reality, a lower conscientiousness, manifested by my weak emotions towards my environment.

I can increase it only when shifting environment to match those same emotions or the ones I wish to manifest.

Everything in our universe is dual, and self-reflected, meaning that we can change our environment with our emotions, as well as change our emotions with our environment.

This principle applies to everything, including wealth.

You produce to gain a salary, as much as you are entitled to use that same salary to produce. In fact, many times you don't even need money to make money. But you do need to create value to get value in return, in the form of wealth, and that's where the law of wealth is rooted.

Likewise, you can improve your mental health by improving the mental health of another person.

This dual law applies also to our interactions. The more altruistic one is, the more this person is clarified by his own actions. And so, we can say that helping another person improves our mental health. That is why volunteering work is so important for those who suffer from depression.

Due to the fact that, historically speaking, people never had many opportunities to create their own destiny, happiness became something we somehow seek and can't find. We got stuck to this idea. But by doing so, we became also more vulnerable to fate.

The solution is then faith! Once one trust his destiny, his destiny will gradually but consistently merge with his dreams, materializing in real life.

There is also an interesting correlation between faith and self-esteem, because people only believe that which the consider to deserve. And so, one won't dream that which is beyond the reach of his potential self-esteem.

If you diminish the self-esteem of a person, you also diminish, to a very great extent, his potential in life. And that is how suppressors, narcissists and emotional vampires, can destroy someone forever, with words only.

UNCOMMON: TRANSCENDING THE LIES OF THE MENTAL HEALTH INDUSTRY

The same applies to how we socialize. We identify only with those who speak in patterns that seem familiar to us. A person with low self-esteem will hardly feel connected with a confident person. They may speak the same language but it will seem like two separate languages.

Chapter 51: Is Happiness a State of Mind?

People are so needy for attention and emotions, that you may seem like a drug dealer to someone you complimented more than what she is used. Especially, when people have low self-esteem, they won't consider if what you say is true or lie, because the gratification of emotional needs becomes a priority.

Humans are born with a positive drive, therefore our low self-esteem is usually produced through negative life experiences or those who suppress us with their insults or discrimination.

Whenever the balance between a positive self-image and a negative one is not moving towards more positive outcomes, our mental health tends to be compromised.

Most of the times, people avoid such situations, by making friends in environments where common agreements are more easily reached, such as a religious congregation.

The predisposition to be angry is actually an attempt at destroying reality in order to maintain affinity with oneself. On the other hand, this leads us to assume that happiness is also related to personal responsibility.

People tend to forget that their results come from a combination of decisions. This makes us able to measure the potential of an individual to achieve happiness by analyzing the capability to compare previously dissociated elements of his life, namely, what he did and what he got.

If you take a white paper and draw two chart in it, one for the things you did and another for the things you got, it becomes very obvious which decisions were dumb and which ones were wise, either they are related to where you have decided to live or the people you wanted to date.

This is why the belief that one can be happy is both an easy and a difficult assumption to manifest; easy in the sense that one is in the command of such outcome, but difficult if we consider that our failures come from our own responsibility.

Not being able to achieve happiness isn't as much a problem of the outside world as it is a problem of the mind operating directly in such world.

Whenever we search for responsible solutions regarding acquiring happiness, even if it is through the accumulation of wealth, we inevitably come to the realization that the fears, as well as the challenges, are all within us and only ourselves. Even our attachments have more to do with us than those we are attached to.

Just because we can't abandon someone, for example, doesn't mean that person won't abandon us in due time.

In any given context, we are not dealing with a problem as much as we are confronting the lack of skills required to solve such problem and that are actually mirroring it, as a problem only becomes problematic if you assume it as necessary. Or, to be more precise, money and relationships, only become a problem when the level of one's needs and the environment satisfying them become incompatible. Reason why even billionaires can have the exact same problems of the middle-class, and failed relationships occur despite any social context or culture.

When people are unable to take responsibility for their situation, they then attack those who mirror that same incapacity. They refuse to agree with anything that forces that responsibility. And so, whenever I explain to people that I worked very hard to have the life I have now, they don't believe, as for them, to agree, means that they would have to accept that they are lazy and stupid.

The need to diminish this reality and make it disappear, although sick, then becomes a predisposition. But such psychopathy has many layers. If you make a person feel stupid for too long, that person may get angry enough to kill you. And here you find the criminal psychopath, that kills to calm his mind, because he can't accept himself. He does murder for this selfish reason, but in his mind, there is no empathy for the victims, because he hasn't acquired empathy for himself either.

UNCOMMON: TRANSCENDING THE LIES OF THE MENTAL HEALTH INDUSTRY

We often assume that self-love and narcissism are the same thing but they are not. The psychopath and the narcissist have to build a fake image of themselves to feel like they can be superior to others. Their crimes, of any nature, are reduced to this obsession to detach from one's consciousness.

They get high only when hurting others, and that's why they can't really be happy. Their happiness comes in a rush of adrenaline, when creating a problem and seeing others angry or panicking. They can only feed from that drama.

It may appear, due to their predicative actions, that they can have responsibility. But that's not really responsibility. It's a self-driven mindset, rooted almost entirely on basic instincts — conflict and sex.

Chapter 52: Why Do We Separate Ourselves From Others?

People have to reject what they can't accept about themselves. It rarely has anything to do with another person in front of them.

This is why, when you do the opposite, and start a conversation by pointing the good qualities of another individual, he will more easily accept your own shortcomings.

For example, most poor people believe that the rich are lucky, because it's easier to accept them this way, rather than to believe that the poor are irresponsible and incompetent in creating their own fate. But only to the extent that their needs are met. As soon as you create a gap, or remove these needs, through unemployment, for example, you increase the potential and risk of violence.

We can therefore affirm that, ignorance decreases the level of affinity with reality, and reality follows that affinity, in the sense that people always find excuses for what which they can't understand. But they never want to confront the reality of "I'm ignorant", and so, they say: "Rich people are lucky and I'm unlucky, and they should pay higher taxes for my life to get better!"

It never happened this way, but most people still believe that raising taxes on the rich, or even murdering them, will benefit the poorest of society.

That's insane because of what such belief implies. But most people have insane and illogical beliefs because they are irresponsible too. They feel entitled to belonging to a society and having a good life, which is an idea that the government gave them to keep the social system working, but never before corresponded to any given reality, or at very least, not in what regards the maintaining of a social system.

You must drive people with an illusion but you cannot keep the illusion with itself.

However, even if you don't say a single word, people can still hate you, if you don't match their reality. Your existence can be offensive to someone if it challenges their belief system.

That same belief system can and does affect the perceptions of reality. People can never see that which they don't want to see.

Most people I encounter, for example, don't believe I write books for a living, because that implies that there is a relationship between working hard and being rich, which, if being the case, means that they are ignorant, as they can't work hard and become rich.

It's easier to believe that I'm not doing what I do, than to believe that they are doing the wrong things and making the wrong decisions in their life, that they have to relearn and change their personality, making decisions that will alter the reality in which they believe and can believe.

The same applies to beliefs on the self. Everyone thinks that they are a good person, and so, when someone else says that they aren't, immediately in their brain they assume that the other person is evil, and everything in the dialogue intends to trap into creating reactions that somehow confirm what they want to believe.

This is why when people do something bad to us, they follow up with defamation and rumors that intend to justify their actions against us. In doing this, the same individual can recover his or her self-esteem.

Many times they will provoke a reaction in us for the same end. E.g., they provoke us in front of others to justify the false image they have spread about ourselves.

Even though free choice and free will do exist, the vast majority of the people do not use their own. They tend to be guided by their own corrupted mind. And yet, while they think that they own their own thoughts, the lack of meditation and introspection, leads us to assume that they don't. For you can't really reprogram yourself if you are not putting conscious efforts in this direction. By default, you always get programmed by your environment and everything that influences you in this same environment, either it is the electric frequencies of your house or the thought vibrations of your acquaintances.

The consequences of this is that beliefs can also make us blind. When we truly want to love someone, for example, we may forgive things that should never be forgiven. And in this sense, we can say that all of our experiences teach us something, as in this case, about ourselves.

In everything we experience, there is a duality manifesting. To observe it from one angle only, is to ignore the other. Any solution then, that comes from a single perspective, is incomplete.

We shouldn't have to force ourselves into balance, but that is often the case. Most of the quotes and mottos that people choose to follow, may seem appealing to the ego, but are not when observed from a double perspective.

One of those, that people love so much is the "work - life - balance" or the "they lived forever happy". Both situations are illusions that can never manifest. Because a balance always results from a lack of it, or that is, the assumption that some things throw you off balance, rather than reinforce this balance.

It would be the same as to say that you can escape problems. Which leads us to the next idea, for you never live forever happy unless you know how to make yourself happy.

We can't expect someone to make us happy if we, ourselves, don't know how to make someone else happy.

Surely, everyone has different expectations and needs, but to be able to be flexible enough to see and accept that in another, is also to be able to recognize that this other may not have the same ability as us.

The student of life must necessarily be a good teacher of it too.

Good fighters don't get anxious over the insults of weak people because they can smell fear. In the same way, a person that knows how to be happy, should not worry about the insults of the miserable, because he is able to empathize with their suffering.

That does not mean, however, that you should try to rationalize with such people, either your position or what you see in them, because their irrational behaviors — or to some extent, unconscious — already show you the lack of potential for that mental exercise.

They would rather kill you than to argue with you. And the way the very stupid murder in modern times is by erasing you and blocking you from all of their social media.

Chapter 53: Does Psychotherapy Have Side Effects?

Whenever people can't accept a reality that is distinct from the one they have formed in their mind, they will use their synapses to fill in the blanks with whatsoever they have in their belief system.

Their beliefs, literally reinforce themselves. And so, as one can't accept that which he has not made real first in his mind, the most ignorant a person is, the most prone this person will be to discrimination, xenophobia and the overall rejection of the greater mass of life and its abstractions. This person will be a brute, limited by the physical world and obsessed with the manifestations of the physical world as well.

We can then say that intelligence and mental health are correlated, for you can't cure the ignorant with consciousness. You can only cure him with drugs and violence — the physical extremes of the physical world.

In order to move one upwards, from the scale of physically towards abstraction, we must be able to also educate this person through the various aspects that education demands. For to uniform education, or to consider uniforming the approach of a therapy as an educational process, would be self-deceptive for these same reasons.

Whenever you equalize the rights, you differentiate the opportunities.

The one capable of an abstract approach to reality will not, quite certainly, manifest the same predisposition as the one that can only believe in what he sees, tastes, feels and accepts.

To make water out of cold ice, something has to break. Within that individual, his beliefs must be broken. But how can such be possible, without a dream, something to aspire for, something that justifies breaking those same inner links?

This is where all of the modern therapies fail, for they do not offer hope, faith in oneself, and a belief in the manifestation of an invisible reality, constructed first within the mind.

Most therapists neglect the imagination and the spiritual aspect — the true self — when seeking for a cure. And that is like trying to find a rat in the woods at night without a flashlight, or to consider that the flashlight can help you find a rat in the woods that is most likely sleeping.

My point is, modern therapy makes sense only for the idiots who trust it. Most of the therapists look like fools trying to teach other fools. For anyone who is not too stupid, can clearly see that the mental health industry of today is a fraud.

I wouldn't expect a psychologist to see himself as a fraud. That is far much more difficult to do, because it implies accepting that the past years of his life where wasted and he or she was fooled. If we could effectively make a psychologist recognize this fact, we would see him or her, turning from therapist to patient.

Every single one of the psychologists I have confronted in my life, runaway from me. They are beaten so badly, in just a few seconds, that they can't handle having their ego thorn apart and so easily.

Going to a debate with me on mental health or education based on the blind beliefs of the academia and the system in which we live, is like trying to fight a dragon with a toothpick.

When such individuals with fragile egos, lose a battle, their mask falls apart, and to restore it, they will position themselves as victims, and label the person doing it as either arrogant, idealistic, selfish or narcissist. They have to always come out with the most dumb excuse to protect themselves from further descending into insanity. Because, indeed, when you destroy the illusions that were part of what another considered to be reality, you dismantle all of his world. It is as seeing reality melting before your eyes. That is very scary!

The attack has to be justified for this reason. The person cannot see what you are doing. Or in this case, me. She is simply scared!

UNCOMMON: TRANSCENDING THE LIES OF THE MENTAL HEALTH INDUSTRY

As an example, I will describe a psychologist I was dating. She thought of herself as very efficient and smart. She was, as a psychologist, very smart indeed. She had several post graduations and many specialties. But she did a grave mistake, when asking me to describe her. Because I did not talk about what she wanted others to see. I talked about what she was revealing about herself behind her beliefs.

I did not insult her, but I made her cry and obsess over this conversation forever. She would eventually move from being in love to hating me forever. Something I was expecting already.

People think they are very strong and able until their arrogance is revealed as a falsehood they took as truth, for lack of a more realistic approach on themselves.

As mentioned before, whenever the therapist lacks the dual perception of reality, not only is she misleading the patient in front of her, but also misleading herself in the process. The two are fooling themselves with this self-deceptive practice.

The way people overcompensate for this problem, if you spend enough time with them, consists of changing you to fit into their paradigms.

Narcissists are experts in this, when they reinforce certain traits of your personality and ignore others. If a narcissist does not respond to your accomplishments, or diminishes them, but is constantly reinforcing your jealousy, suspicions and feelings of lack of self-worth, you will soon find yourself acting as if you were insane.

This leads us to another aspect of the dual reality that is hard to deal with, and it's the fact that many of the people we love or loved, have made us insane. Their own insecurities, fears and beliefs were somehow passed unto our subconscious mind.

Chapter 54: Is Self-Absorption The Root of All Psychological Evil?

Over the years, I have come to the realization I can't really say what I do to most people because they cannot understand it, and will spend their time trying to justify something that they can't accept.

A person that wants to become a writer and can't do it, for example, only has two options: Either she enjoys spending time with me, and learns with the interaction, or can't accept my personality, and creates an alternative reality to justify her own incompetence and protect her ego. That new reality will have to consist in diminishing my value. My need to keep it, will turn into a war of egos.

Whenever you find yourself having to prove something, as in showing your awards, accomplishments and references or reviews from others, you are already losing this battle. You are descending to the level of stupidity and egotistic weakness of the other person. You shouldn't need to experience this, if that person was able to understand you, from your own viewpoint, and at the very least, empathize with you.

If I show to someone acting like this that many of my books have become best sellers, for example, she will call me arrogant, or say that those who bought them did a mistake, and didn't know what they were purchasing, or that the success made me blind to the truth. And as crazy as it may appear, I got many of such attacks from other fellow authors who can't sell anything. Rather than acknowledging their lack of value, they project it, and try to diminish mine.

As for those who can't associate my personality with that of an author, they will try to make me confess something that isn't real, such as that I steal knowledge from somewhere or someone. They will do this through many childlike tricks. Even if I say that other people inspire me, that can easily be shifted in its meaning to the idea that the knowledge was stolen from such people.

Once the person has made her belief true, it doesn't matter what I say next, because their reality is justified and sealed already.

Another thing that people may do to protect their ego, although less common, is to project themselves above you, as when saying: "If I was in your situation, I would do things differently!"

In my case, people often say, for example: "If I was an author, I would write more pages, and work with different publishers."

They think that their answer is logic or realistic, while it's just how they deal with the fact that they may never write even a single book in their entire life.

People typically do the same when talking about relationships. They always think that they know more than others about love and happiness, because they are unable to introspect and look at the limitations of their own mind.

It is very easy to see this once you become wiser than the majority of the population. That's when you realize they have no clue of what they are saying, but insist on it like a religious mantra. Their ego is deeply rooted in such imbecility.

It is not a coincidence, nonetheless, that the more rooted someone is in delusional beliefs, the more likely this person is to be drunk all the time. Drugs and alcohol, among which we can include antidepressants, are other forms of avoiding a confrontation with both reality and the ego.

What we call 'negative thinking' is actually made out of this same avoidance. A person always labels as negative that which she can't accept. And so, whenever someone avoids problems because she thinks that is 'negative thinking', she is actually labeling as 'negative' to be more mature about life. That is why the many self-entitled 'positive thinkers' seem like little children trying to chase soap bubbles.

Whenever such individuals have to confront a very high level of reality, they label it as negative, if they can't do that. That is why, while many doctors say that my books are enlightening, there are some poor souls that will say: "Lots of serious mistakes."

UNCOMMON: TRANSCENDING THE LIES OF THE MENTAL HEALTH INDUSTRY

Saying that my books have lots of grammar mistakes, when they only found one or two, is how they reject the whole information that they couldn't process, assimilate and understand.

I remember one person in particular who suffered severely from this egotistical mindset. She was a scientist, and so, grew up hearing people tell her that she was very smart. Her ego was so solidified, that she couldn't handle her own failures. She used to ask me often to read tarot cards for her, which I did, as a special favor. And then, she would tell me that my predictions did not come true, because her relationships failed, as if I was to blame for her own behaviors.

I met one of her former boyfriends and invited him for lunch, trying to understand the gap that was missing between what I saw and the stories she told me. And the guy was quick to tell me that she cheats, is disrespectful and selfish. He didn't say it this way, but described me behaviors that are clearly unacceptable, as in flirting with many other men all the time, and meeting with them to test the value of her hypergamy.

You see, she was so egotistical, that she was always searching for a better partner, and that's exactly why she couldn't keep any. She was the one self-destroying the relationships by not accepting any. As soon as she got the guy she wanted, she would consider if she could get better.

You have certainly met many women like this. Even men. But what makes this story interesting, is her obsession with trying to solve a problem that she, herself, was creating.

When she came to the conclusion that I wasn't falling for her illusions anymore, she started denying my own reality, saying that she understands my own books better than I do.

That is probably the most ridiculous thing anyone can say to a writer. But it shows you how far anyone can go when wanting to protect their ego.

Narcissists, in particular, are so delusional about themselves, that they do this on purpose and all the time. They have to deny themselves responsibility by gaslighting another person, with phrases like, "That never happened", "That is the past and I am a new person now", "That is what you think", or "You don't know the whole truth".

They just can't accept the fact that they are horrible people. The worse on the planet. Therefore, they spend an entire life blaming the entire world for what they do, reinforcing even more their tactics and obsessions.

The narcissist goes through life never changing, but getting worse, more aggressive, more obsessed with control, and more paranoid about being abandoned.

Their relationships get shorter and shorter, while they seek for weaker and weaker victims.

The victim isn't necessarily a victim, because there is a transaction occurring. But it often feels like a diabolical transaction. For any ugly man feels validated with a very beautiful woman that may steal his soul and life savings in return, and divorce him too. And any woman without self-esteem will feel validated with a rich and handsome man that may abuse her physically and break her heart multiple times with the worse insults.

Chapter 55: How to Protect Yourself From Emotional Abuse?

In psychology it is said that the mind is divided in three levels — Superego, Ego and Id.

The Id is related to instinctive behavior and the superego is the conscious you. In other words, the ego is the part of your persona that manages your instincts and your conscious beliefs.

When someone attacks you, the normal reaction is to have a response, and people respond in different ways, according to their instincts. If your instinct has plenty of guilt within it, then that's what you feel. If your instinct tells you to fight back or cry, then that's what you do.

In therapy, a psychologist or psychiatrist acts as the superego in order to modify the habit, while the Id maintains its presence as the unconscious or instinctive self, reacting in a certain way because of habits built in the past.

From a therapeutical point of view, anyone can become anything, if you rebuild the Id with new habits (Ego) in a conscious way (Superego), but most people are so attached to their old habits, that they don't change and can't accept a change within themselves. And yet, the opposite of being a victim consists in being in control of one's life.

Life is a system of cause and effect, so you're always either more cause or more effect over your life.

The more in effect you are, the lower the level of your presence within reality, which eventually affects your health as well, not only psychologically but also physically.

The higher you are in this scale, the more in control you are. The two things are correlated. Which means that, if you do things that you can control, you gain more happiness. And, if you learn to control other people, as in making them feel happier, you also feel less of a victim of your circumstances.

This is why everything starts and ends with communication. As a matter of fact, if you develop your capability to analyze others and their intentions, while building your happiness in social interactions, you're already positioning yourself in a much better situation from a healthy standpoint than the vast majority.

You will eventually realize that there are certainly people in the world that we should be avoiding. They're usually identified as emotional vampires. These are individuals that, despite our efforts and good intentions, insist in consuming our vitality and disintegrate our happiness. And surely, identifying them is as important as being openminded in our social interactions.

One of the most common strategies that such personalities use is based on guilt, namely, offers that cannot be paid back, such as an expensive trip that is offered.

Another common strategy consists in stripping the victim of any defenses, by isolating him or her from friends and spending his or her money to create more vulnerability and dependency.

This is often done covertly, such as with hints that provoke disagreements and misunderstandings between the victim and his or her friends and relatives.

Nonetheless, such behaviors aren't possible without first collecting information about the victim in regards to what makes him or her happiness or sad.

These type of situations, in which someone is afraid to be happy or sad because of the reaction of the emotional vampire, creates emotional codependency and vulnerability, which the aggressor then uses to make the victim feel helpless or incompetent.

The only way possible of dealing with such personalities consists in confronting them with their actions and abandoning them as a form of punishment, which is actually the worse they can receive.

Only then can the dynamic of power invert, allowing to push through some demands related to accepting therapy, if and only if they do accept it, which is usually not the case.

UNCOMMON: TRANSCENDING THE LIES OF THE MENTAL HEALTH INDUSTRY

On the other hand, with every abandonment, the victim also trains himself or herself to detach and become less codependent, later facilitating his own total detachment from toxic situations. It is and can be seen, as a form of mental training, in which we learn to protect our emotional resources.

Chapter 56: How to Properly Judge People?

For most of us, analyzing who is trustworthy or not, who can be a potential spouse or, on the contrary, a criminal or a psychopath, remains a very difficult task. The common person doesn't really know how to detect psychopathic or sociopathic traits in others, and much less detect a highly moral and ethical individual.

This difficulty creates challenges of a various nature. But how can we properly evaluate someone if we, ourselves, are not properly educated on the concept of moral — right and wrong.

To be moral means to respect norms and principles. Therefore, one of the characteristics of morality is that it must be perceived under certain guidelines. And one isn't moral until he understands them.

For this purpose, there's an interference of rationality, as one must choose either responsibility or irresponsibility over his conduct.

The ability to rationalize misconduct is equal or superior to the ability to rationalize proper conduct, because the one that goes against the moral of a group knows that he must outsmart his own group to actually be immoral.

On the other hand, it is as difficult to understand why one should be moral in his actions, as it is to find reasons to blame others, for there are paradigms in both cases that shape our vision of reality.

The concept of good and evil is well present when we're 3yo and even before. Turiel believed that children can actually differentiate social norms from moral, and in doing so, know what is wrong and what is evil. But one of the greatest challenges we face growing up, is the realization that to be just we may have to be unjust, and in order to be protected against evil, we sometimes need to act in an evil way.

Such paradox positions us in conflict with our own values, forcing us to redefine them constantly.

It is for this reason that moral tends to be relativized. People do not have equal patterns of understanding in regards to what is good or bad, and even though we can create a hierarchy of values and priorities, from the most egotistical to the most altruistic.

Besides, we cannot forget that different cultures may have different perceptions over the same facts, and what they consider to be moral or not.

The common paradigm that can be observed in these cases, concerns the reasons behind what is considered or not to be normal.

Before an act is considered immoral, one must question the reasons that are justifying it. And then, according to the reasons behind the act, we can proceed to create levels of morality:

1. Normative - We shouldn't do something;
2. Utilitarian - We shouldn't do something because we can get caught;
3. Equalitarian - We shouldn't do something because it creates inequalities;
4. Perfectionist - When we disobey laws that are against humanitarian rights for equality.

As a matter of fact, we can say that the most highly moral individuals are those who follow a certain perfectionism, often placed above what the vast majority can perceive as right or wrong.

They are the revolutionaries, fighting for things that others aren't even aware to need, such as the right to freedom, to the truth and to justice.

On the opposite side, we find the majority, usually succumbing to normative or utilitarian ideals, following laws that they don't, can't and won't understand, simply because they were told this is how they must behave.

These, I must say, are the least trustworthy among us, the more prone to criminal acts, if provided the right environment and conditions. Under the right circumstances, they can legitimize their immorality, such as when nobody else is seeing what they do and say.

UNCOMMON: TRANSCENDING THE LIES OF THE MENTAL HEALTH INDUSTRY

We find here everyone that appears to show different masks, in public and when at home with their spouse.

Chapter 57: Can Society Contribute to Poor Mental Health?

The believers in social learning agree that moral conscience can be learned through a direct absorption of the patterns valued by the social environment. In this case, moral development would be a direct result of the interaction between the individual and his equals. The individual will judge his own moral acts by how it affects others, or most of the people around him, rather than the nature of the act itself on a larger scale.

We have here the application of moral as being an assimilation of what the individual perceives to be right or wrong.

Due to the implications of such fact, many experts have suggested that moral shouldn't be put in a hierarchy, but rather analyzed according to the context. For one may consider to be morally correct to do something evil if the social environment consents it.

We also know that, very often, the act of not acting, is in itself a demonstration of a moral act, such as when one remains silent or passive before another human being in suffering or dying.

In this case, we can indeed question those that selfishly believe that belonging to a religious community is enough to erase their responsibility over the rest of the world, or judge those who, despite not committing criminal acts, do not try to stop anyone when having such chance, and do not try to stop criminals from doing injustice to others.

This is to say, it is as immoral a bully as everyone around him permitting his act on another human being. And this makes us responsible by default for everything occurring in our society. For it is as guilty the bully that hurts a child in school, as the children that, upon observing, do nothing about it, or the parents of those children that, when knowing about it, also do nothing about it, because it is not their own child the one involved in the altercation.

The same principle applies to suicide. It is true the premise that nobody dies alone.

Whenever a person is suffering from depression, sadness and emotional suffering in general, everyone that knows about it and doesn't interfere positively, is indeed responsible for the consequences that such individual imposes on himself, as much as they are responsible for the consequences that such individual brings back to society, when turning into a criminal.

We can't say that a person is moral until such individual understands it from a personal standpoint and applies it accordingly. In other words, one can't truly be moral until he is himself ethical. And being ethical means understanding moral from a personal viewpoint, independently of the approval or disapproval of others, or even their criticism.

Now, why is it that adults can't be ethical?

Until 9yo, a human being doesn't really understand the difference between external and internal morality. Up to this point, behavior is based on fear, obedience and unilateral respect for authority, rather than self-conscious acts. And one can question if adults still operating in the same way, have actually developed beyond the age of 9, or still, generally speaking, think like a 9 yo. Because, from the studies of Piaget and others, we know that independent, or autonomous morality, only occurs after 10yo. And it's based on mutual respect, cooperation, equality and social agreements. Here, social norms have been interiorized and absorbed by the cognitive nature of the individual.

The difference between both situations finds itself in how the ego is handled. Whenever one is more egotistical, he finds it hard to position himself on the viewpoint of another person. On the other hand, without this capacity, one naturally develops fears associated with segregation and rejection, which inevitably make him more egotistical in nature.

The ability to think as another person or from another person's position, has the name of Morality by Heteronomy, and is moved by a force external to the individual, as explained first by Immanuel Kant

UNCOMMON: TRANSCENDING THE LIES OF THE MENTAL HEALTH INDUSTRY

He characterized heteronomy as the capacity to think from many different perspectives, being healthy socialization, with compassion and empathy, the practice that will allow this development.

Therefore, we can assume that lack of empathy, in the vast majority of the population, is a sign of mental retardation. People's aren't just stupid, but literally retarded, in the sense that they can't really understand the meaning or importance of being moral.

Chapter 58: What are The Stages of Moral Development?

The most important change in a child occurs around 10yo, when the child moves beyond the concept of immorality, as associated to punishment, and into a subjective immorality, violating the spirit of reciprocity and cooperation.

It is not until a child is about 10yo, that she will understand moral as associated with a group. In fact, if there is no immediate punishment for a rule that is broken, the child may even consider herself immune to moral transgressions.

We can very well say that those who have been wrongly punished or not punished at all while children, may more easily develop immoral behavior. And even though we may only assume it, a stretch in our conclusions leads us to see neglect from parents as one of the causes leading to psychopathy.

Only between 22 and 25yo, do people develop a post-conventional morality, associated with universal principles, like the right to life. And this is the type of moral that society needs to survive as such.

The Internalization of Moral Values, as developed by Kohlberg, is divided in six levels of development:

Level 1 - The Moral of Punishment: The individual in this stage guides his behavior based on obedience and punishment.

His level of obedience is proportional to the consequences he gets for not following certain rules.

Here, morality is confused with punishment, and barely understood as such. It's only considered wrong what leads to punishment. And the perception of it tends to be obtained through physical means rather than emotional.

We have here all those who stretch the boundaries of their insults and rudeness, until they get a punch in the face. Or the criminals, that only stop when in jail.

These are the psychopaths and mass murderers of society;

Level 2 - The Moral of Interest: Here, actions are considered correct or incorrect according to how much they allow fulfilling personal desires. Morality is seen as an exchange for practical purposes and, therefore, the individual judges behaviors as moral or not according to what gives him the most gains.

In this level, people may be polite, for example, to their boss, because he pays them a salary, or to their clients, to get money from them, but not to anyone else.

This is the levels of the hypocrites and opportunists;

Level 3 - The Moral of the Heart: In this stage an interpersonal moral emerges. The individual understands moral as being associated with a group and worries about social norms, even though his analysis is related to an emotional relationship with others, rather than a perception of their own good and needs.

These individuals are worried about social approval, rather than necessarily what is and not good.

Many artists and singers are in this level. They behave according to what others perceive as right or wrong. We can even extend this group to include those who want to be popular;

Level 4 - The Moral of the Law: At this stage, the individual puts his trust in the law as a necessity to keep social order. These individuals have the ability to coordinate different perspectives and needs under one single judgment.

These are the people that completely trust their governments to tell them what is right or wrong;

Level 5 - The Moral of the Relativism of the Law: This stage, usually manifesting around 20 to 25yo, represents an understanding of the relativism of the law, especially, when it is in conflict with universal principles.

The moral of these individuals is here seen as a freedom to express unity and altruism. They perceive freedom and the right to life as being above any others.

UNCOMMON: TRANSCENDING THE LIES OF THE MENTAL HEALTH INDUSTRY

The main motivation of these individuals is a transformation of society towards higher goals, instead of the maintenance of the social rules as they are in present time.

These are the non-conformists, the whistleblowers, the political activists, the writers that seek to change the world with their words, and so on.

Up until this stage, we can already notice how very few people have reached what could be considered a normal and civilized level for a human being. But let us proceed, for the last level, where you will barely find anyone, is the sixth.

Level 6 - The Moral of Universal Reason: At this level, the individual has a moral compulsion and feels a moral need to do what is correct and should be seen as correct by anyone. He transcends the moral levels of others, by assuming responsibility for them. His conscience rules over punishments or even social laws. And he considers people as an end rather than a means

This is the level of ethical behavior and altruistic actions, when one does what is right without thinking about benefiting from his behavior in any way, or even while aware of the consequences of it, including the loss of his own life.

This is the level of those who risk everything, including their reputation, their finances and their own survival, to share the truth with others.

Chapter 59: How to Evaluate Moral Development?

There are three ways to evaluate moral development:

- The Psychoanalytic Approach evaluates moral development through the feelings of guilt after the transgressions, how individuals show more or less empathy towards others, and how willing they are for altruistic acts, once they recognize their fault or responsibility in the actions;

- The Social Learning Perspective, believes that people should be measured by how frequently they engage in moral or immoral acts. What the individual thinks about himself or his acts has little importance. Those who follow such perspective believe that the more the individual operates on moral acts, the more moral he will tend to be — the habit and not consciousness, forms the individual;

- The Cognitive-Developing Perspective, considers that only through reason can we judge others' actions, but also judge them as moral or immoral. This idea complements with the educational belief that the more knowledgeable people are, the more civilized, and consequently, empathetic, they will be towards others.

We could consider the first perspective as being focused on introspection, the second as being related to behavior learning — as in copying what is seen, and the third as being rooted in reason and wisdom.

These perspectives do tend to find more or less prominence depending on the perspective taken. Because the first approach is typical of religious congregations, and yet, we can't say for sure that the people are motivated by a moral intent to do good more than than the avoidance of punishment.

Countless studies have shown that the pressure of a group is stronger than the individual's will for either good or evil, as the individual can be coerced to do one thing or another, depending on the hierarchy and motivations of the group in itself.

Here, we find the examples of the cults that lead to either murder or suicide, as well as those who explore their members' beliefs to enslave them in the name of voluntary work.

The third approach is better judged through our universities. The consistent implementation of political ideologies inside the educational system, has led to a massive brainwashing that, in current times, has proven to be dangerous to the stability of the social system in itself as well as our democracy.

Socialistic and communists ideologies have shown us a new type of fascism, in which the rule of the sheeple, brainwashed by hidden powers, controls and overrides reason and even moral.

In the name of peace and equality, the masses are now willing to kill. And that, in itself, invalidates any of these three approaches.

How can we then judge others?

If we compare these perspectives, we will notice a parallelism between three elements — empathy, reason and behaviors. To be more precise, we can differentiate two types of people as being the first more motivated towards moral acts, and the second more selfish and orientated towards their own ego.

The first type will show more kindness and willingness to help others, and also empathy for the emotions they perceive in other people. They will be more susceptible to help those in need. But the second type, will clearly show a drive towards selfishness. This type of person justifies her or his actions based on personal needs and doesn't rationalize the needs of others or completely ignores them. Consequently, the majority of his or her actions are immoral, offensive and hurtful.

UNCOMMON: TRANSCENDING THE LIES OF THE MENTAL HEALTH INDUSTRY

Now, while an altruistic driven person will justify her behavior with something like "I did it to help the other person", the egotistical individual will probably give more answers along the line of "He deserved it" or "I didn't have a choice".

In other words, even though a highly moral person thinks about the preservation and survival of human beings, including himself, the immoral individual neglects even the consequences of her own behavior, and operates on the idea of punishing the other. And this occurs in such a way, that the immoral one cannot process responsibility or even see herself as responsible when in a conflict of interests.

Her lack of ability to comprehend the other, to be empathetic to his emotional needs, makes her naturally selfish, and evil by default. And this evilness is a consequence of not being able to be responsible.

We see then that both responsibility and morality are correlated in the answers of both types of persons. For while one type combines responsibility to justify moral behavior, the second type denies such responsibility, and rather transfers it as a form of justification.

In resume, the moral one prioritizes ethics over behavior, while the unethical acts first and justifies later, by trying to assimilate morality into his actions, and not the opposite.

This is why narcissists, by being egotistically driven, always act without thinking. It is in their nature to do first and think later, to cheat first and explain why later, to blame the other for their actions, to shift blame to society as a whole if necessary, or even to their past. Whatever is the cause, can never be found in themselves.

The altruistic are able of long term thinking and planning, because they adjust their actions to the moral laws of the society in which they live. Reason why they are social beings, contrary to narcissists, who are typically, for the reasons presented here, antisocial.

The narcissist may have many friends and be a very popular person, and yet, be antisocial, if not obeying any form of rule, either implicit or explicit.

The narcissists are loyal to nobody, but their own desires. And for this reason, they tend to be abandoned by everyone — lovers and friends.

As a result of abandonment, the narcissist becomes more needy, for validation, attention and emotional support. Therefore, the abandonment they receive opens a wound in them and causes more suffering, namely, by exposing their deepest fear — the fear of loneliness. And this is precisely why narcissists always get worse in time. Their fear consumes them entirely.

Their narcissism gets stronger because so does their shame and lack of self-esteem become more overwhelming and unbearable.

The altruist, on the other hand, by being able to build stronger relationships and being persistent on his or her plans, is more likely to succeed, and build a stronger self-esteem out of that success.

In a way, and due to these reasons, we could say that both misery and happiness are the result of our own karma. And so, moral is not dissociated from success, happiness, or even long term consequences (or karma), and our self-image and confidence. Everything is related.

Chapter 60: What are The Effects of Immorality?

When we talk about psychopathy, we're basically dealing with individuals that are incapable of processing guilt, remorse or responsibility; individuals that can't assume any role on the suffering they inflict on others, either it is emotional or physical.

Many times, these individuals are operating not even on the basis of what they observe, but what they think and want. Such is the case of a woman that was hurt by many men, and then hurts one that didn't hurt her back, and justifies her actions by his reactions.

Whenever a person can't feel empathy for another being, we have the moral ground for the development of psychopathic behavior, I.e., beliefs, actions and thoughts, based on previous traumas rather than reality.

The psychopathic person is insane because she is unable to see reality as it is, and not as she thinks it is.

One becomes psychopathic when his mental world is the only real world, despite what occurs outside of it. That's the best definition of insanity.

When one thinks he knows without knowing, and can see without seeing, that is when he is truly insane.

Now, even though there are different opinions on this topic, many experts believe that social interactions and parenthood have the most important impact on our development. And although it's possible to change and affect the moral behavior of someone, this change is always based on a system of reinforcements of certain actions, which isn't always possible if the individual is exposed to different or opposing values.

Education can also affect how the individual is influenced by his environment, as his cognitive development will determine his potential to develop or not a higher stage in his moral development.

The two, cognitive and moral development, are interconnected, for a person needs to understand the implications of his actions before he can see them as moral or immoral.

For this reason, many experts believe that a child can be directly educated for moral behavior, and indoctrinated into behaving a certain way, if the child can understand the implications of a bad action and the rewards present in good actions.

This stimulation of the intellect and the reasons behind moral behavior is what can stimulate the individual predisposition for kind acts.

This ability can be acquired as well by promoting discussions between different parties.

An adult, can develop his moral reasoning by learning to consider the perspective of others, either in meetings or her own relationship. The more we can accept the differences between us and others, the more we can perceive the meaning of having empathy and moral.

This is why Kohlberg believed that moral development will eventually show a capacity to differentiate, integrate and put different perspectives into a hierarchy of opposing values, which will inevitably force the individual to uncenter himself from his egotistical needs, and in doing so, detach from the lowest levels of moral to embrace the highest.

Hoffman considered that social behavior is, nonetheless, affected by the relations at home. Parents that tend to control their children by using and abusing physical power, or to punish them, or by retracting in their love without properly explaining their behavior, can have very serious and damaging impacts on the moral development of their children.

If a child isn't induced to process what is right or wrong, to discuss it, to explain herself, that child may grow up to become an adult with a very low level of moral. Therefore, it is believed that in order to promote moral development, children must be educated more for thought than knowledge, and have opportunities for expressing their self-respect, to consider different perspectives, and to assume responsibilities within an environment of justice.

Several researches have proven that there's a relation between moral actions and moral thought, meaning that criminals have a lower perception of moral, even when related to their own group.

What these results also tell us, is that there's an indirect correlation between moral and cognitive development, which means that a proper education can indeed affect the moral behavior.

They show us that moral reasoning is more important than an education for moral virtues, that understanding what moral is shows itself more important than simply accepting moral values.

Along this line, forgiveness appears to be an attribute of people with compassion, those that are willing to suspend their judgements in order to accept one whom they've condemned. In this sense, those that can forgive are the same as those who have the highest moral standards, which means that the same behavior can't be expected from the ones they often forgive in a time in which reciprocity is expected to come to both.

Chapter 61: How to Be Uncommon and Moral?

Along the path of our existence, we must develop a certain ability to channel our ambitions and egotistical wants, while respecting the same right in others and controlling our own emotions in interactions that show us the differences.

This need for a "transformation" and "alchemical change" in heart and mind, will then make us better persons, not just for others, but also ourselves.

- To forgive the shortcomings of others, is to be able to forgive ourselves for ours;

- To be patient towards the imperfections in others, is to allow them to learn to tolerate ours;

- To be expect the best from others, is to make them expect the best from us too.

People tend to reflect back that which they feel. And so, as we learn to become better versions of ourselves, we push that level of expectation on others too.

The arrogance and jealousy that we may feel coming from others always says more about their limitations than ours. For most people can't debate things beyond their comprehension. They get scared, as if afraid their fantasy world could collapse to pieces. And it's that resistance that show us the level of fluidity of their thoughts. A type of fluidity that we must develop within ourselves to be able to adapt and change, without compromising our own values.

As an example, I have always been very open to all religions and ideologies, but at this point in my life, I get easily restless and frustrated, although I actually believed that with age I would be more patient. The opposite happened! Because now I feel a greater sense of restlessness and urgency.

Money or reputation mean nothing to me when compared to time. Without time, the rest means truly nothing. And if I see my values clashing against a wall of egocentrism, I lose interest in the people who are forming that wall, as they stop the fluidity of my character and, in doing so, make me lose time.

I always expect more from people, and so should you, even when that is rarely found. It is the only way you will ever find the best people among the worse. To practice good expectations is to keep your level of discernment in the highest stage possible.

It is the invisible element of the world that pulls us forward and not the visible one. The visible aspect of life will turn us inwards instead.

We all have a path to fulfill, that may or may not encompass the ones we know, but as you evolve, the vast majority of the people around you will see you as maladapted, and even crazy, as if you had no idea of what you are doing.

They judge very lightly without even looking at the reasons and mostly from the limitations of their own ego.

You don't need a specific goal in life but you do need to maintain values, in order to be resilient to the challenges you face.

Among such values, the most important is freedom. But I have noticed that for most people freedom is something rather abstract. They don't really know what it means.

I treasure the freedom to work as much as I want, in what I want, and where I want. But for the majority of the people, this is irrelevant. That's why many enjoyed the lockdown of 2020. Many were even happy to be in house arrest. And this was the main reason as to why I lost many friends during this period. I didn't insult them, but made it clear that I thought it is stupid to consider that as a great moment to meditate or stay at home and rest.

I think a person needs to be mentally ill, to see in a lockdown, motivated mainly by political reasons, an excellent moment to meditate. That's like saying to the Jews that the Nazis helped them become more united and return to their roots in Israel.

UNCOMMON: TRANSCENDING THE LIES OF THE MENTAL HEALTH INDUSTRY

A lot of the sickness of this world comes from this need to justify evil or insane practices, when generalized.

I respect differences of opinion. The problem begins when a person talks to me from a pedestal of moral superiority.

I can understand that everyone has its own path and we are all in the same path somehow, but then I start wondering what's my purpose among those who reject this differentiation and try to impose a superiority, that quite frankly, they don't have, at least, not in what regards their relation to me.

Whenever such people realize who I am or how much I have done in my life, they panic, because their sense of entitlement is shattered to pieces and they realize the truth of their imbecility.

It is not very relevant for me what others perceive from what I do or where I am, or even who I am from a social standpoint, but I am willing to work 16 hours a day, every day, to have the freedom to choose to work in what I want, and only with whom I want. And I've noticed most people can't handle that, they can't recognize the level of effort one puts to be free. All my relationships collapsed due to my strong determinism, and friendships too, also fell apart because most people can't understand this.

I can certainly say that now, when I look back at my life experience, everything is connected and made me who I am today. But, at the same time, I can't say I knew what I was doing. I had no idea!

This is why I insist so much in telling you that your values are far more important than your results will ever be. You are what you represent to yourself and not what you represent to others or what happens to you.

Also by Dan Desmarques

Spiritual Warfare: What You Need to Know About Overcoming Adversity
Collective Consciousness: How to Transcend Mass Consciousness and Become One With the Universe
The Spiritual Mechanics of Love: Secrets They Don't Want You to Know about Understanding and Processing Emotions
The 10 Laws of Transmutation: The Multidimensional Power of Your Subconscious Mind
The Evil Within: The Spiritual Battle in Your Mind
Deception: When Everything You Know about God is Wrong
How to Change the World: The Path of Global Ascension Through Consciousness
Religious Leadership: The 8 Rules Behind Successful Congregations
The 14 Karmic Laws of Love: How to Develop a Healthy and Conscious Relationship With Your Soulmate
A New Way of Being: How to Rewire Your Brain and Take Control of Your Life
Uma Nova Forma de Existir: Como Organizar Sua Mente e Assumir o Controle da Sua Vida
O Propósito da Sua Alma: A Reencarnação e o Espectro da Consciência na Evolução
Your Soul Purpose: Reincarnation and the Spectrum of Consciousness in Human Evolution
Encontre Seu fluxo: Como Adquirir a Sabedoria e o Conhecimento de Deus
Find Your Flow: How to Get Wisdom and Knowledge from God
66 Days to Change Your Life: 12 Steps to Effortlessly Remove Mental Blocks, Reprogram Your Brain and Become a Money Magnet
66 Dias Para Mudar Sua Vida: 12 Etapas Para Remover Bloqueios Mentais, Reprogramar Seu Cérebro e Atrair Dinheiro

Consciência Coletiva: Como Transcender a Consciência de Massa e Se Tornar Um com o Universo

Batalha Espiritual: O Que Você Precisa Saber Para Superar a Adversidade

Codex Illuminatus: Quotes & Sayings of Dan Desmarques

Codex Illuminatus: Citações e Provérbios de Dan Desmarques

As 14 Leis Cármicas do Amor: Como Desenvolver Um Relacionamento Saudável e Consciente Com Sua Alma Gêmea

The Hidden Language of God: How to Find a Balance Between Freedom and Responsibility

Your Full Potential: How to Overcome Fear and Solve Any Problem

The Secret Science of the Soul: How to Transcend Common Sense and Get What You Really Want From Life

?????????????????????

Technocracy: The New World Order of the Illuminati and The Battle Between Good and Evil

The Secret Empire: The Hidden Truth Behind the Power Elite and the Knights of the New World Order

The Antichrist: The Grand Plan of Total Global Enslavement

Holistic Psychology: 77 Secrets about the Mind That They Don't Want You to Know

Uncommon: Transcending the Lies of the Mental Health Industry

About the Publisher

This book was published by 22Lions.com.
    Follow us at Facebook.com/22lions

www.ingramcontent.com/pod-product-compliance
Lightning Source LLC
Chambersburg PA
CBHW072000070526
44583CB00015B/1268